PALACE OF STRANGERS

JAMES EARLE

He who seeks truth should be of no country.
Voltaire

ISBN: 061586726X
ISBN-13: 978-0615867267

O LORD, Thou art my God;
I will exalt Thee,
I will give thanks to Thy name;
for Thou hast worked wonders,
plans formed long ago,
with perfect faithfulness.
For Thou hast made
a city into a heap,
a fortified city into a ruin;
a palace of strangers
is a city no more. . . .

Isaiah 25:1-2a (NASB)

CONTENTS

PROLOGUE

Who will, may hear Sordello's story told.
Robert Browning (1812-1889) *Sordello*, bk.i, l.1

In the pensive years following the daunting surgical intervention, I pondered the notion. It is, after all, a patently observable phenomenon. Few so fearfully examined by the slings and arrows of outrageous fortune emerge without alteration. Because we're not dominoes given to falling over in rows, this alteration takes varied form, occasionally quite remarkable. Perhaps surviving calamity, one may experience a quickening by which he is endowed with – not necessarily an enhanced capacity – but an animated willingness to gaze beyond the torn veil that continues to separate God and man. Perhaps by acknowledging the uniformity of our broken existence, the stagnant air of long-abandoned catacombs may once again be flushed with life-giving force. And perhaps, having avoided the Stygian crossing, the serendipitous pilgrim may yet live, and live abundantly, glimpsing once more – at long last – the mesmerizing epiphanic Jesus.

INTRODUCTION

It is not in the storm nor in the strife
We feel benumb'd, and wish to be no more,
But in the after-silence on the shore,
When all is lost, except a little life.
Lord Byron (1788-1824) *On Hearing Lady Byron was Ill*

Only now, after the deluge, have I begun to fathom the magnitude of the delusion, and it has become as a fire in my innermost being, and I cannot hold it in.

A fine ambition, the quest for truth, and its promulgation a sober responsibility; but truth's composition is as hazardous and volcanic a fulminate as any man can lay hands upon. Only the Christian expatriate with nothing to lose and everything to gain is truly free to mine and assay truth wherever it may be found, whether among believer or disbeliever, cleric or excommunicate, or even – as Emerson thought – in the perception of the soul whose just relationship with the divine spirit makes profane the interposition of helps.[1]

I know now that success does not emanate from hard work or victory from an abundance of character. Neither are fame and fortune, by force of circumstance, bestowed upon honorable men and virtuous women. If these childhood assurances had possessed any measure of legitimacy, the worn Elijah Roy would have died a rich, favored old man instead of a poor, broken White River Bottoms cotton farmer. And the supermarket tabloids would be out-of-business, which, as can be seen, clearly they are not. These truths being self-evident, the modest station of the prophet provides no grounds for rejection of his truth . . . and truth is no less truth, even if spoken by the devil himself.

*

Although the last-ditch surgical procedure which salvaged my life was technologically explainable, its success was without doubt a remarkable accomplishment by a skilled team of professionals assembled from around the world at a modern medical Mecca known as Presbyterian-University Hospital, Pittsburgh. The staff who manned that station was, however, well-grounded in reality. They knew – as Anna and I learned – that the effort failed more than occasionally and its early successes left wide-open the lubricous issue of quality-of-life.

I neither did then nor now subscribe to the supposition that everything happens for a purpose, but every significant happening can be and often is put to a purpose. Whichever then, by design or fortuity, I survived the surgery and in its aftermath became inheritor and caretaker of a most unorthodox theory. The theory provides a plausible answer to the most perplexing and frequently asked theological question of our time. For who among us, scorched with great heat, has not raised his hands to God, who has power over the plagues, with palms up in prayerful entreaty . . . or fists clinched in angry blasphemy?

From those who profess knowledge of divine philosophy to the totally alienated, whose dwellings have ranged from the ramshackle hovels of Mississippi River Delta sharecroppers to the shaded mansions of auspicious plantation owners and their vested sons and daughters, all have more in common than they care to admit. There are frogs in kings' bedchambers and the death angel cannot be bribed. Malady and misfortune, tragedy and mishap sprout among the luckless and the fortuitous, the seemingly cursed and the presumably blessed, like poisonous weeds in the furrows of a field. For the ill-fated, whatever their socioeconomic status, the dominant mood of the day isn't joy but, as the sage knew, a profound sense of desperation. In a world poised at the threshold of the third modern millennium, one encounters mankind-in-despair nearing the apogee, where the comfortable expect the impossible, the destitute await the improbable, and neither lives as though anticipating anything beyond the grave.

Certainly, in the beginning, there was provided an effectual solution . . . or so we've been told.

*

Rich and various gems inlay
The unadorned bosom of the deep.
John Milton (1608-1674) *Comus* (1634), l.22

I was a proper candidate for succession to the theory. Since childhood, I'd suspected the answers to the questions which perplex modern man lay not strewn upon the sandy beaches of his future, as high school valedictorians often suppose, but embedded in the granite bedrock of his past. For me, the solution to the riddles of the present and the secret to the promise of the future rested quietly entombed within the labyrinthine record first laid down on skins and parchment with pen and ink. And in the sluice of that thoroughly unexpected survival at Pittsburgh, that puerile suspicion did at last come of age.

The revelation didn't come by direct divine infusion, at least as that experience is popularly envisioned. It came instead by the *willingness* to consider the heretofore unthinkable.

*

What soul was his, when from the naked top
Of some bold headland, he beheld the sun
Rise up and bathe the world in light!
William Wordsworth (1770-1850) *The Excursion* (1814), bk. i, l.198

We are but dwarfs on the shoulders of giants. If we see more clearly than they and to a greater distance, it's not because of superior vision, but because we are lifted high, elevated in our perspective by their prior experience.[2] The theory suggests the written record of the ancient Hebrews – that alchemic melding of history and prophecy that is their venerable legacy – provides just such a platform.

In giving substance to the theory, there's no intent to disturb those who are at ease with current explanations for that which they daily observe and experience. Those who are at ease hold calamity in contempt. But for those who despair of senseless hardship and tragedy, for those possessed by a gut-wrenching desire to know why God allows bad things to happen and why these bad things – as often as not – happen to good people, the theory offers admissible explication.

*

If you know from whence you began and where you've been, you can ascertain where you are. And knowing where you are, you – unlike many others – have the power to choose where you are going. So do the right thing. Begin now to be the pilgrim, the seeker that you will be hereafter. Consider the evergreen laurel I call "the theory," its apical flower, which I call "the still point paradigm," and the paradigm's venerable antithesis, the fortified sanctuary the prophet Isaiah called a "palace of strangers." Then, having done all, whatever your conclusions, go in the strength that comes from knowing.

A brave world, Sir, full of religion, knavery, and change:
we shall shortly see better days.
Mrs. Aphra Behn (1640-1689) *The Roundheads*, I.i

John Ward Eakins
Springfield, Missouri
Autumn, 2012

CHAPTER 1

THE EPIPHANIC JESUS

Diseases desperate grown, by desperate appliances are reliev'd, or not at all.
William Shakespeare, *Hamlet,* IV.iii..9

Pittsburgh, Allegheny County, Pennsylvania
September, 1988

Anna and I had asked for and received permission to visit the transplant unit prior to completing check-in at the admissions desk on the first-floor. Panic welled up in my throat and lodged there like a splintered chicken bone the instant the elevator doors opened directly onto Presbyterian-University Hospital's tenth-floor unit designated 10-B. The intensity that met the eyes and flooded the auditory and olfactory senses was palpable. I stiffened and attempted to choke down in a single, strained gulp all there was to imbibe in that gravid moment.

There were many, many persons crowding the wide hallway. All were attempting, by various means, to maneuver around each other, the medicine carts, and other portable medical equipment that jammed the hallway. Some, dressed in appropriate staff attire, moved crisply and neatly, weaving in and out of the morass of human and mechanical debris. These were the doctors, nurses, and aides. The rest were made up of a ghastly cadre of stooped individuals, men and women of all ages. These moved cautiously up and down the hallway, shuffling their feet as they went, tethered by transparent tubes to the IV poles that each clung to and pushed before them. The majority of these patients were wear-ing in identical thin, loose-fitting, cotton-print, hospital-issue pajamas. The scene reminded me of the newsreels of hapless Nazi concentration camp victims I'd witnessed as a boy immediately after the close of the war. Like those poor, tortured souls, these were – for the time being – the successes. God help the failures.

The wide doors to the patients' rooms were kept open for the convenience of the staff. The scenes a stranger could witness through those open doors were shocking to one as yet uninitiated in the desperation that accompanies life and death on such a unit. That desperation saturated the very air we breathed. It was heavy, laden with anxiety and the smell of numerous chemical and biochemical substances. It smelled like death.

When desperate illness demands immediate remedy, doubts are an unaffordable luxury and caution an unmitigated absurdity. I knew I had to swallow the reservation I had regarding what lay ahead, but I may as well have been trying to gulp down a thumb-sized screw.

In the months preceding the Pittsburgh experience, reality had leapt ahead with great, consuming strides while my mind stalled to ponder the significance of each infinitesimal tick of the clock. Unlike the hare, reality never paused and snoozed, allowing my plodding psyche opportunity to catch up. I would forever toast the grim experience with the wine of astonishment. But I never anticipated its anomalous residuum, for that which began with a miscarriage of the body did, in its proper season, conclude with a metamorphosis of the mind. And that which commenced with a lame, halting descent into the valley of the shadow of death did, at last, blossom into a most remarkable hope.

* * *

Springfield, Greene County, Missouri
September, 1988

It was late summer or perhaps early autumn. I wasn't sure. The concentration required to consider such a question was exhausting. After all, fatigue and confusion were end-stage symptoms of the condition. I sat motionless that morning in the pale gold recliner beside my window on the world. Gray early morning light penetrated the sliding glass door to my left and scattered throughout our small, comfortable living room. A steady rain had fallen late the previous afternoon and throughout the night, leaving the lawn flecked with pale green and yellow leaves that lay soaked and lifeless on the recently mown grass. The hours of continuous rainfall had saturated the trunks of the mature oaks in the backyard, tinting them almost black. Leaves still on the branches glistened and continued to shed large drops of water in the umbrae of those great arboreal canopies.

The green, luxuriant trappings of summer were fading. Sunlight was diminishing, the estival clouds fleeting, Anna's summer plants showing signs of withering – all this poignantly reflective of the autumn of my life. And then, of course, there was the rain.

Although the condition had left me uncertain of the day, I could even then read the face of the sky, and I was certain of the time. It was September. The season of growth and maturation had ended. The harvest was at the doorstep, and winter followed after. The rain had revealed it to me.

I'd learned to recognize the autumnal rains in the warm glow of a golden childhood, growing up in the flat, agriculturally-rich row crop country of northeast Arkansas, an hour north of Memphis on U.S. 61. According to my father, a farm real estate salesman *par excellence*, our native Mississippi County topsoil was sixty feet deep and more productive than any this side of the Nile River valley.

The weathered cotton farmers – that grizzled cadre of firm personae who provided our community with its *raison d'être* – were responsible for my precocity in the matter of the rains. Their oscillatory, meteorologically-dependent economic fortunes effectively dominated conversation at every dining table, cafe and general store throughout the year. For the farmers, an early onset of the autumnal rains brought a grim urgency to the cotton harvest. But in the innocence of a radiant youth, I eagerly anticipated the rains. I found them to be the harbinger of wonderful things, autumn things, to come.

*

He that but once too nearly hears
The music of forfended spheres
Is thenceforth lonely, and for all
His days as one who treads the Wall

Of China, and, on this hand, sees
Cities and their civilities
And, on the other, lions.

Coventry Patmore (1823-1896), *The Victories of Love*, bk.I.ii.
From Mrs. Graham, l.15

The equinoctial rains possessed a signature that escaped me neither in that idyllic springtime of my youth nor on that poignant September morning. Summer storms, you see, arise suddenly and dramatically, furiously flaying the redwood deck and thrashing the august oaks that stand immediately beyond my window on the world. Then they subside, their retreat as rapid as their advance. Their visit is brief and sharply delineated. Immediately before and after the summer storms, there is bright sunshine and familiar warmth. But it is not so with the autumnal rains. With these, there is instead a solidly overcast sky and a moderate, steady rainfall that continues for hours, perhaps tens of hours. And a gray, lingering chill follows after.

The rains of September produced a soft, hypnotic patter on the redwood deck beyond the sliding glass door, a narcotic tattoo that penetrated the deep recesses of the mind. From the pale gold recliner before my window on the world, I'd watched with fascination the day before as raindrops peppered the flooded deck. I'd sat there, mesmerized as in my childhood by the mental image of tiny, brave soldiers rising up from the puddles to do battle, only to immediately fall and disappear. Vanishing into the placid constancy that gave them birth, they left nothing to mark their brief existence, nothing to show they had ever really been there. And that rueful observation was never want in resurrecting its replicate, for there was kinship between the raindrop soldiers and the forgotten dead surrounding the solitary young warrior who stood on a Tennessee hilltop in another, more distant autumn. That was a different time and place, when the seasons stretched out interminably and the mother lode from which they issued seemed inexhaustible.

It had been later in the season then, following the first hard freeze. The sky had been similarly overcast, the ground similarly wet from recent rain. The damp, chill wind had rattled the brim of my gray felt Stetson and rustled the stiff, brown leaves still clinging to the nearby scrub oaks.

I'd been alone that day, too, standing in the middle of an abandoned, early-nineteenth-century country cemetery. No roads then in existence came within four-hundred yards of that isolated site. I wouldn't have known it was there had I not noticed the slight irregularity on the recently flown, high-resolution aerial photographs I carried in the cab of my pickup truck. It was part of my job, inventorying all real estate construction in Middle Tennessee's Marshall County, checking out and recording a description of all structural anomalies that appeared on those aerial maps.

I'd stood alone that day among those aging, lichen-covered tombstones, pondering the encrypted epitaphs placed there generations ago. Just who were these people whose birth and death were so carefully preserved in the stone, yet the marrow of whose lives was now forgotten? That they lacked the greatness of thought or deed that conferred spontaneous immortality was apparent, but surely they'd had something lasting to contribute to the chronicle of man. Whatever that may have been, it was now lost forever in their waveless passing.

I'd stood alone that day, surrounded by the sentries which guarded their eternal rest. For decade upon decade, that clustered garrison had whispered to distant, inattentive ears. But that day, I'd heard. Having lived and breathed, their light now extinguished in darkness, they were remembered no more than the fallen sparrows of those yesteryears. This is not how man should live and die.

The Soul that rises with us, our life's Star,
Hath had elsewhere its setting,
And cometh from afar;
Not in entire forgetfulness,
And not in utter nakedness,
But trailing clouds of glory do we come
From God, who is our home . . .

William Wordsworth (1770-1850), *Ode. Intimations of Immortality* (1807)

Disturbed by raindrop soldiers, haunted by forgotten spirits, what did that say about me then? That I wanted to live, or at least leave some tangible mark? Of course I wanted life and purpose. That desire is a function of man's intellective quantum leap over the highest of the higher animals. It's his magnificent intellect that is evidence of his eternal soul, for man is fearfully constructed in the image of the gods.

His thirst for immortality is an intellectual necessity, a longing born of the immutability of an eternal spirit. For man, death simply isn't natural.

A charm
For thee, my gentle-hearted Charles, to whom
No sound is dissonant which tells of Life.
Samuel Taylor Coleridge (1772-1834) *This Lime-Tree Bower my Prison*, l.74

Ten-year-old Jared had left a half-hour earlier, walking to his fourth-grade class at Sarah Barnhill Elementary School. The public school building was only a few hundred feet away, as-the-crow-flies, out the backyard gate and across the canopied back lawn of the Immaculate Conception Catholic Church. Anna had left for her last morning's obligations in the front office at Belmont Convalescent Center. She would be doing little more at the office that morning than confirming responsibilities already reassigned to others and receiving the well wishes of co-workers. Our hastily contrived plans, born of necessity, were all in place. Anna would return about ten-thirty that morning, in the same hour that Jared would be briefly excused to come home from school. He'd be accompanied by his older sister, Rebekah, who would be coming from the university campus across town.

Rebekah was grown now, a senior at the university, where I was on the faculty. She would look after Jared; Ming, the family's aging Pekinese; and the house during Anna's and my absence.

The dispatcher at City Cab Company had been asked to have a taxi in the driveway at eleven o'clock. Two large suitcases were already positioned in the foyer, awaiting the driver who would be asked to give assistance with them. The noon-hour flight to St. Louis and then to Pittsburgh would be the end of the search for remedy. God knows the search for cause had taken long enough.

Before leaving that morning, Anna had leaned over my chair to kiss me good-bye and softly inquire if there was anything left she could do for me. That was so much like the incomparable Anna. I'd signaled her there was nothing I wanted. She'd crossed the room to the entrance foyer and then to the front door, turned to blow me a kiss, and smiled faintly as she turned and closed the door behind her.

I'd waited with anticipation, following the sound of her footsteps on the pavement, listening for the dissonance which would mark the opening and closing of the station wagon door, followed by the engine ignition. I'd audibly measured the car's movement down the driveway, the shifting of the gears, and the Doppler effect created by the engine noise as the car moved away. As much as I loved Anna and delighted in her company, I had at that time an intense need for silence. At last, I felt the enveloping silence, sluiceway to the abysmal heart.

I looked about the room and listened intently, carefully dissecting the sounds that reached out to my still keenly attentive ear. There was the rhythmic, almost imperceptible respiration of the old Pekinese, sleeping as he was, reposed on the floor at my feet. There was the distant, gentle whine of the refrigerator in the kitchen. And there was the measured cadence of the wall clock in the foyer. I scanned the redwood deck and the landscape behind our modest suburban dwelling. The rain had stopped, but the overcast sky and high humidity had kept the deck damp. Prismatic droplets of water beaded on the tightly-spaced parallel straps that formed the backs of the deck chairs.

I carefully observed the almost indiscernible motion of the leaves and branches of the mature oaks lining the yard and dotting the manicured, twenty-two acre landscape of the church which lay immediately beyond our low, chain-link backyard fence. But I heard not a whisper of the force that stirred them. I was insulated within the confines of that room, warm and protected within the shell born of forced retreat, anesthetized within the womb to which I had returned. It was, after all, characteristic of the condition.

At last, as I'd anticipated, I heard in the distance the tumult of the children exiting to play during the first morning recess at the school.

I'd often anticipated the distant sound of the children's laughter and shouting, for it had a way of settling upon my ear like the sound of enchanting, symphonic wind chimes. From the pale gold recliner beside my window on the world, I could see the children's teachers on the playground with them, directing play like stripe-shirted referees at a varsity basketball game. The teachers wore whistles around their necks and, like camp counselors, used them frequently. Their irksome blasts on those disagreeable whistles were a noisome pollutant, tainting and staining the sounds of my childhood that drifted across the decades.

Lulled in the countless chambers of the brain,
Our thoughts are linked by many a hidden chain:
Awake but one, and lo, what myriads arise!
Alexander Pope (1688-1744)

Merged into the stillness that surrounded me, becalmed by the specter of an imminent, ghastly death from uncontrollable variceal hemorrhaging, like some ancient mariner adrift on a glassy sea, I wistfully fixed my gaze in the direction of the children. Their gaily colored attire and frenzied activities produced a soft, kaleidoscopic blend of color and pattern as my eyes focused on an invisible point between the playground and my reclusive perch. And as the discordant playground sounds metamorphosed into an arresting harmony, it all came back to me. As though traveling backwards in time, borne through the eons by some incorporeal Jules Verne time machine, I returned by the agency of the mind to the beginning. Captured by the sights and sounds of youthful exuberance that flooded my senses, scenes burned into the memory of a rural Arkansas lad growing up in the years immediately following the war lit up my flagging consciousness, surreal incarnations like the flickering images of an old silent movie. I could see it! I could feel it! And for a fleeting moment, I smelled the distinctive fragrance of new crayons.

* * *

Study the past if you would divine the future.
Confucius

The theory suggests man can, by the recovery and mapping of his past, uncover secrets of the present and the future. This is not dependent upon powers magical, mystical, or miraculous, but the recognition that the macro-history of man is not open-ended, as most casually suppose. It is rather, as some of our advanced theories of the universe, a closed circuit. This doesn't imply that individuals have personal destinies to which they are irrevocably assigned and which cannot be avoided. Every individual remains free to come and go, to be or not to be, as the individual so chooses. But the theory does maintain that mankind, by his very nature, is locked into the spiral of a collective destiny. This destiny is not one assigned by a capricious, malevolent spirit being – God, if you will – but a destiny dictated by inherent characteristics peculiar to man, characteristics that were manifest in their entirety as early as 930 B.C.E.

How charming is divine philosophy!
Not harsh, and crabbed as dull fools suppose,
But musical as is Apollo's lute,
And a perpetual feast of nectared sweets,
Where no crude surfeit reigns.
John Milton (1608-1674) *Comus* (1634), l.476

Now divine philosophy may be for some a vast and trackless ocean, but I was accorded an early introduction to the ancient Hebrew record referred to as the Old Testament. That this particular segment of the written record is so provocative and engaging is no mere coincidence. There is a genius in this collection that defies a ready secular explanation. There is layered intelligence in this ancient compilation, structured like the leaves of an onion. If through learning, acuity, and diligent application the potential of the record seems exhausted, there is an unexplored level waiting beneath, and so on, *ad infinitum.* This characteristic becomes most absorbing when one is aware of the background and history of the collection – perhaps a hundred different authors, perhaps a thousand years in the making, yet at the core it has a cohesiveness that, despite variations in style, suggests singular authorship. The documents fit together as though intended for ingestion as a single unit – as though one should swallow an eight-pound melon . . . whole.

*

Leona Landon was a writer of children's books, a Connecticut Yankee who in the autumn of 1947 visited Mississippi County, where I was born and raised. She was researching a children's book about that rural Mississippi River Delta country and its people. In the forward to her book, published in 1949, she penned a succinct, effectual description of the country as she saw it in the autumn of her visitation. She referred to it as "another and a different world." [3] She was right, of course. But it wasn't only that provincial, Mid-Southern locale and its autumn cotton-pickin' time that was so extraordinary. It was the era.

Immediately following the surrender of the Axis powers, America had stood astride the world like a colossus. American servicemen on furlough showed up for their Saturday night dates wearing their service uniforms – even in rural Arkansas. It garnered them that much respect. Abroad, Americans and their American dollars were respected and valued. Now, in the wake of a series of inundations that have swept away the last vestiges of childhood innocence, that time and place remain for me singular and exceptional. It was, after all, the time and place of my first encounter with the epiphanic Jesus.

I'd always been able to summon on command a veritable flood of trivia from the tense, dramatic World War II years and the euphoric post-war era that followed. But the condition that was overwhelming me in mid-life – that rude, premature initiation into the twilight zone between life and death – occasioned the ascendance of a particular incident from that era. The encounter with the epiphanic Jesus was a happening that I would come to fully understand only much later, in the borrowed years following the encounter at the Stygian crossing.

* * *

Who reads
Incessantly, and to his reading brings not
A spirit and judgment equal or superior
(And what he brings,
what needs he elsewhere seek?)…
John Milton (1608-1674) *Paradise Regained* (1671), bk. iv, l.322

Skeptics dismiss this ancient record on the grounds that its interpretation is fathomless. Thus divisions and factious wars, some hot and many cold, are part of its heritage. But diverse interpretations of a static record over hundreds of years needn't make divisiveness a characteristic of that record. Perhaps that divisiveness is a characteristic of man that's being adroitly exploited by a fathomless intellect. What if the construct of the ancient Hebrew record is far advanced beyond a ready understanding, as some theorize of the great pyramids and temples of antiquity? What if the record is not a transmitter, as is simplistically supposed, but a transponder, designed to transmit a given message only upon first receiving a designated signal. If that be the case, the ancient Hebrew record presents as the product of a most complete understanding of the nature and limitations of man, a static presentation with a message called truth, targeting man's thorniest questions . . . but with a perceived message that is a function of the inquirer. If this be the case, what response could legitimately be expected to such a record? Peace and unity, or war and division?

Not unexpectedly, war and division are observed. From the ancient Hebrew record springs a fountainhead of dissension – some Jewish, some Islamic, some Christian, and from these spring Jewish divisions, Islamic divisions, and Christian divisions. Much the same can be said of that which has been laid down complementary to the record – the Jewish Talmud, the Islamic Quran, and the Greek language collection of first-century letters and essays called the New Testament.

Perhaps the record's ability to expose the capricious, often malevolent content of the human heart is testimony to a most unexpected attribute. Perhaps the design is not intended to unite, as is supposed, but rather to divide along characteristics inherent in man – as would, say, a sword.

What you believe will depend very much upon what you are.
Noah Porter (1811-1892)

In his quest for truth, what man finds most readily is a function of what he already is. If he's evil, truth presents as evil. If he's good, truth presents as good. If he's ruthless, truth presents as ruthless. If he's a fool, truth presents as foolish. And if he's materialistic, well, take a wild guess. Reveal one's perception of truth you reveal a facet, not so much of truth, but of that specific individual. When understanding is colored by such disingenuous bias, the table thus set becomes a snare. When one fills himself from such a table, that set table becomes a trap.

If a man has made up his mind that a certain mistaken course is the right one, the more he follows his conscience, the more he becomes committed to his conviction. Such a man may even find himself serving his enemy conscientiously. And the steel trap closes. The blind end up leading the blind, and both are fallen into similar misfortune.

Misunderstanding is more problematic than indifference because misunderstanding is active. Indifference (or neutrality) is effectively a blank sheet. Misunderstanding is a scribbled one. There's simply much further to go in retracing one's steps before one can even conceive of a different train of thought. There were some present on the Day of Pentecost who achieved this – but only after they had unwittingly crucified the Christ and then were eyewitness to a most remarkable demonstration of the Holy Spirit.

But what if one is a newborn babe? The newborn babe is the perfect blank sheet. There's nothing to distort truth, no pre-existing mold in which to force truth, nothing to be gained or – even more importantly – lost by the essence of truth. There's no great mystery to it. To such a one, truth – however abstruse it may seem to others – presents simply as truth. Perhaps during our lifetime, one is never closer to God than at the moment of birth, and man's sole purpose is to return to the open-minded simplicity of that earliest state, in effect, to be born again and, like virgin parchment, receptive to an original inscription.

The theory holds this is the operational genius behind the ancient Hebrew record, a Southern Oracle ferreting out the impure of motive with a piercing gaze directly into the heart. If this is the case, the search for truth in the ancient record can lead to truth only if truth is the unfeigned desire of the soul, as it is instinctively to a child. All others, rich or poor, noble or ignoble, wise or simple are ensnared by their own inherent predilections in a weave so fine, so creative as to bend the mind as light is bent by enormous gravitational force.

What is seen then is not so much man probing this ancient document for truth as it is this ancient document probing each individual for that once untainted mindset. Religion seeks after God, but the theory holds the ancient Hebrew record is God seeking after man.

Awake, my St. John! Leave all meaner things
To low ambition, and the pride of kings.
Let us (since Life can little more supply
Than just to look about us and to die)
Expatiate free o'er all this scene of man;
A mighty maze! But not without a plan.

Alexander Pope (1688-1744) *An Essay on Man,* Epistle i, (1733), l.362

It is a mighty maze and an inventive plan, but the theory submits the creative genius forging it implanted keys within the mystery. These keys lead beyond the maze to the greater understanding. In accordance with the profundity of the plan, these keys are imaginatively recessed, resisting – by design – the cursory review of the falsely motivated and the marginally concerned.

Mankind will never achieve recovery of the keys because of the inherent limitations of collective man. Individuals and small, eclectic groups, however, may indeed lay hold of the keys implanted within the mystery and thereby lay claim to knowledge – and perhaps divine favor – which has been submerged, for all practical purposes, since at least the fourth-century. The record even indicates such groups may number anywhere between two and about one-hundred adults.

* * *

In 1938, the secular Chester Eakins and the fundamentalist Christian Helen Roy Eakins moved the family residence from the Missouri Bootheel to the small farming community of Osceola, Arkansas, about thirty miles south. By the early '40s, home was a twenty-five-dollar-a-month, two-bedroom, one-bath cracker box on North Pearl Street in Osceola. That house, decent and attractive in its time, was one of a row of such houses that could've been stamped out by the same cookie cutter.

Osceola was at that time absent any tangible representation of Helen Eakins' inherited religious denomination. This twist of fate provided her with the opportunity to become a charter member of "the church" in Osceola.

He loves his bonds, who when the first are broke,
Submits his neck unto a second yoke.
Robert Herrick (1591-1674) *To Love*

As a small boy, I attended the initial Sunday services of the church in the dimly-lighted auditorium of one of the town's two motion picture theaters. There were only a few attendees, mostly women and children. The preacher – that indispensable, omnipresent staple of modern Christianity – was a rotund and jocular sort I knew only as Brother Billings. He commuted from Memphis each Sunday in exchange for little more than the traditionally magnificent Sunday dinner at the home of a favored parishioner, or so I understood. This situation existed only briefly, however, for the first item of business for the fledgling church in Osceola became the hiring of a resident preacher and the construction of a small, but distinctive meeting house – a church building.

Thus it came about that immediately upon coming together, the little congregation of the church at Osceola set out to burden themselves and their expressed missionary and benevolent outreach with the iron yoke of debt service, building maintenance, and payroll obligations.

It would escape my attention for so many years. Only decades later, with mind and body adrift amidst the debris created by the condition and the unanticipated survival, did I attach any significance to that seemingly innocuous sequence of events. Only decades later did I come to suspect in that familiar dyad the signal characteristics of a grand design carried awry and a sublime potential unrealized – and all with the best of intentions.

The simple bird that thinks two notes a song.
W. H. Davies (1870-1940) *April's Charms*

In the decades that followed, that hallowed brace – construction and staffing – was buttressed by childhood recollection of adult events and actions undertaken with full and complete social and clerical sanction, swimmingly accepted as an integral part of mainstream Christianity. This became in my mind a matter of no little consequence, for the theory holds that in this cardinal orientation lies explanation for the most persistent and perplexing theological question of our time.

***

The day becomes more solemn and serene
When noon is past -- there is a harmony
In autumn, and a lustre in its sky,
Which through the summer is not heard or seen,
As if it could not be, as if it had not been!
Percy Bysshe Shelley, *Hymn to Intellectual Beauty* (1816)

In that other and different world of my golden childhood, autumn was marked by the distinctive fragrance of the summer's collection of lint being burned off the furnace when first fired, a season when migrating birds following the great Mississippi River flyway swarmed at multiple levels. In the alfalfa fields, teeming blackbirds landing and taking to flight created rippling waves resembling that of ripe Kansas wheat. High overhead, dozens of magnificent southbound V-formations of migrating geese tracked across the autumn sky.

By Labor Day, the annual invasion of migrant workers had begun. There were jobs picking cotton for migrants and locals alike. On every Saturday evening during those days of cotton-pickin' time, families of locals and migrant workers from all over the county converged on Blytheville, the county seat eighteen miles north, for the spending of the week's wages. On those bustling evenings, the wide sidewalks of the downtown's Main Street business district were so crowded with humanity that pedestrian traffic spilled over into the street. On those Saturday visitations to Blytheville, Helen Eakins allowed me to browse the sectioned tables of merchandise at S. H. Kress' Five-and-Dime Store. It was there that I first beheld the epiphanic Jesus.

It was a small plastic rectangle similar to a picture frame, but thicker with roughly the same dimensions as a penny postcard. I held it in the palm of my hand in front of my face as I would a mirror, but it wasn't a mirror. Where I expected to see my reflection, there were only thin, closely spaced, wavy lines running horizontally across the face of the frame. There were no instructions, nothing to clue the viewer what to expect of this object. Staring quizzically into the herringbone maze, attempting but failing to perceive my image, any image, it suddenly materialized before my startled eyes!

The epiphanic Jesus was not some supernatural visitation of the resurrected Christ. It was instead an unexpected portrayal that came into focus where previously there had been nothing but blank curiosity. It was similar but not identical to an optical illusion, for there was indeed substance to the epiphanic Jesus. The representation came and went, and came again, but each time more swiftly and distinctly, for I progressively acquired a better understanding of the nature and character of the representation and came to anticipate its advent. And so it was with each successive attempt to visualize that which had previously reposed just beyond my totally vacant first impression.

By most clever design, the epiphanic Jesus was eventually visible to the steady stare of all those possessing desire and a modicum of patience. But it remained consistently imperceptible to the oblique glances of the marginally concerned and the decidedly disinterested. The image, when perceived at all, was simply the spontaneous consequence of a conjuncture involving a constant (the cleverly designed representation) and a variable (the candidate possessed of genuine desire and modest aptitude).

Why I'd been able to stare into the face of the object, yet fail to perceive the image, I cannot say to this day, even with the recent reemergence of 3-D art. But once having perceived the image, from that time forward it readily materialized to my then trained and expectant eye.

I purchased the toy I later came to call the epiphanic Jesus, but not from any motive that might be considered religious. I simply found the art form fascinating. All to whom I showed the toy experienced the same initial difficulty I'd experienced. Some perceived the image more quickly than others. Some initially attempted to visualize the image, but becoming impatient and nonplussed, quickly dismissed the whole thing as silly. Others, never accepting that the image was there in the first place, summarily dismissed the possibility. Thus, whether through transience or disbelief, these never saw the image. And if that bothered them, it was never apparent to me.

None of my toys from that era survived the years and the subsequent family relocations. My three-tracked Lionel electric train set, kaleidoscope, Red Rider BB gun, marble collection, and the epiphanic Jesus – all have been gone for many years now. But the lesson of the epiphanic Jesus remains etched in my memory.

Decades later, I would once again experience the phenomenon of the epiphanic Jesus. But this time, I would be looking squarely into the maze that is the ancient Hebrew record. Only then would I perceive in the record the grand archetype that had been there all along, awaiting the pilgrim who would approach as a curious, receptive child with no notion of what he was supposed to find.

CHAPTER 2

DRIV'N BY THE SPHERES

I saw Eternity the other night,
All calm, as it was bright;
Like a great ring of pure and endless light,
And round beneath it, Time in hours, days, years,
Driv'n by the spheres
Like a vast shadow mov'd; in which the world
And all her train were hurl'd.
Henry Vaughan (1622-1695), *The World*

Chester Eakins was twenty-eight years old when he went off to war in the summer of '44. He'd been able to stay out of the war until then because he had a wife and two children and had enlisted in the Arkansas National Guard. But by 1944, the wartime draft was threatening to make him an infantryman. Perceiving he could in some measure avoid the danger and hardships of jungle warfare in the Pacific and the hazards of the anticipated invasion of the Japanese homeland, Chester Eakins enlisted in the Navy.

Chester was as capable as any of engaging in those long, after-supper, front-porch, all-male colloquies involving war and politics, but he was not a hothead. He wasn't the type to rush off to war and get shot in a spate of patriotic fervor. He was an outdoorsman, a hail-fellow-well-met and – modestly – a family man, but he was first and foremost a salesman. Having only a high school education, he was a man of extraordinary, if unpolished, social skills. Using the contacts he made as a farm implement salesman at Cartwright's Hardware and Farm Implement Store during the early years of the war, he established the base for his post-war success in selling farm real estate.

After boot camp at Camp Wallace, Texas, he returned home on furlough before reporting to his first naval station in Seattle. It's among my earliest childhood recollections. We didn't go down to the Frisco railroad depot to see him off. I stood on the front porch of the five-room cracker box and watched him walk away in his Navy whites, duffel bag slung over his shoulder. He crossed the street and, looking back just once, disappeared around the hedged corner of the Cartwright mansion one-half block away. The lump in my throat closed off my voice as effectively as a garrote. Helen Eakins cried for weeks.

* * *

The theory is grounded in the awareness and knowledge of cycles. The physical world, seen and unseen, from the smallest particles of matter to the great galaxies, is prescribed by cycles. Beyond these, seasons and years come and go and come again. That which is born dies, but not without seed, which in its appointed time gives birth again. A generation comes and goes and comes again. The sun rises and sets, hurrying to its place where it rises again. The wind swirls out of the north on its circular course and returns to swirl out of the north again. Rivers flow to the sea to be taken up into clouds, fall as rain, and flow to the sea again.[4] These observations are part of the heritage that is the ancient Hebrew record. And they lie at the foundation of understanding, or so their author thought.

There are great long cycles, such as that exhibited by Halley's Comet. This body is composed, as all matter, of myriad atomic particles with electrons orbiting nuclei, yet is itself captured in rotation around the sun. And the sun is in turn held within the greater rotation of our galaxy – cycles within cycles, a wheel in the middle of a wheel.[5]

Since childhood, I'd understood the seasonal cycles, and the lunar phases were in no way inscrutable to me. In my case, knowledge had taken the mystery out of processes that to ancient man bordered on the divine, as indeed they may. But what remained for me to contemplate were the relatively recent and unmistakable cyclical patterns in civilized man's communal history, oscillations of social rather than natural phenomena. The natural cycles had been there from the beginning, but social cycles required the ascent of man.

The universe may be billions of years old, and modern man may be one- or even two-million years old. Civilization, however, that stage of social and cultural development by which the great riverine societies of Babylon and Egypt arose concurrently with the advent of writing, is only about six-thousand years old. According to the theory, it was the simultaneous, interrelated advent of writing and civilization at the dawn of the fourth millennium B.C.E. that activated mankind's seven-thousand-year clock. But that's another story for another time

Civilizations, political movements, reformations, and revolutions all exhibit recognizable life cycles, some extended, some compressed, often one within another. Historians have pointed to distinct generational theories in Anglo-American and world history. Cyclic (or wave) theories persist for a very good reason: they fit the observations.

> **The thing that hath been, it is that which shall be; and that which is done is that which shall be done: and there is no new thing under the sun.** Ecclesiastes 1:9 (KJV)

In the 1920's, Russian economist Nikolai Kondratieff published a theory that business activity in the major Western nations assumed a rhythmic wave pattern over relatively long periods. Kondratieff's theory held the pattern reflected the cumulative force of human nature, that is to say, a new generation repeating – even if in a different form – the mistakes of its predecessors.

Cyclical patterns do not imply some divine force that predestines the future. The stimulus is quite mundane. For example, the prediction of approximately one-hundred fatalities on the nation's highways tomorrow is a sound, if regrettable, projection based upon observable human behavior over a long period of time, but it needn't be realized unless man wills it. The daily fatalities experienced on our nation's highways could be reduced to zero (or near zero) on any given day or series of days, but that scenario is dependent upon every driver obeying all traffic laws and driving courteously and defensively for the same twenty-four-hour period. It's theoretically possible, but it won't happen. It won't happen because such unified, cooperative action is not in the nature of man.

There's room for exception, but only for the individual. Every individual remains free to come and go, to be or not to be, to spend tomorrow in his bed, if he so chooses. But the theory suggests collective man, by his very nature, is locked into the spiral of a collective destiny. Inherent characteristics of man dictate his collective future, not the gods.

*

I know now there are recurring patterns in the ancient record, patterns that never before came to my attention, an orbiting of consequential circumstance to be seen and grasped that no would-be guide of mine ever acknowledged. Perusing the tomes of dry biblical history which so readily anesthetized me in my youth, I no longer saw sterile history, but vibrant prophecy – prophecy disguised as history.

As though a great map covering many tens of acres, the ancient record reveals the completed chronicle of man, his past, present, and future. But just as with the Peruvian lines to the mountain gods at Nazca, the map can't be recognized, much less interpreted, from the limited perspective available at the level of the plain. It must be espied, if at all, from that apical headland which makes distinct the epiphanic Jesus.

* * *

Doubtless the pleasure is as great
Of being cheated, as to cheat.
As lookers-on feel most delight,
That least perceive a juggler's sleight,
And still the less they understand,
The more th' admire his sleight of hand.
Samuel Butler (1612-1680) *Hudibras*, pt. II, c.3, l.1

In the autumn of '44, Helen Eakins, my sister Jean and I followed Chester Eakins across the country to Seattle. Helen was twenty-eight years old. Jean was nine. I was five. Spending days and nights on trains crowded to capacity with uniformed soldiers, we traversed the great American countryside from northeast Arkansas to Chicago and then across the Great Northwest.

Wartime rail traffic was heavy with westbound war material receiving higher priority than passenger carriers. Our packed train was frequently sidetracked as long, serpentine freight trains snaked ahead through the twisting canyons and mountain passes. These magnificent freight trains were perhaps one-hundred cars in length, with scores of them identical black oil tanker cars loaded with fuel bound for the West Coast. These trains had multiple steam locomotives in tandem on the front, another in the middle, and another pushing from the rear – all these great iron horses belching black smoke from their stacks as they crept up the grade in that magnificent, serpentine column.

I don't presume many American families made such odysseys during the war. I'm certain there was only one other civilian on that train and that was a young woman traveling without children. What possessed Helen Eakins to elect such an impractical choice, I've never fully understood.

The great majority of the soldiers were amicable and kindly disposed to Helen Eakins and her two children, and spending entire days and nights together on a slow-moving, crowded train crossing wartime America did on occasion breed warm familiarities. At those times, soldiers from the adjacent railroad car would come and invite Jean and me to join them. When once again ensconced in their niche, these likable warriors would perform magic and card tricks for us, thoroughly bedeviling Jean and me. But the soldier's legerdemain that most fascinated me was not one readily duplicated by any of his comrades, despite any amount of time and practice, for it was a performance born of a natural endowment. Skill lay only in the judicious choosing of his props, carefully timed and executed distraction, and, perhaps most especially, the choosing of his audience.

This soldier and his sycophantic entourage always sat in the most desirable seats, the first such brace of seats in the car. He always occupied the position next to the window on the forward-facing bench. Upon my most earnest plea, this soldier would have one of his ready assistants remove a light bulb from one of the overhead fixtures in the railroad car. Spreading his white handkerchief wide in his lap, the soldier would place the light bulb in the handkerchief and close the corners, thus being able to wield the bundle like a blackjack.

With startling suddenness, the soldier would shatter the light bulb with a hard rap against the window sill. He would then bury his face in the opened handkerchief and emerge with bulging cheeks. This thespian soldier would then begin to munch – and the sound that accompanied his mastication was precisely that of fragile glass being ground between the teeth! A big and somewhat strained gulp, a mouth opened wide for inspection, and an empty handkerchief provided the final proof.

The slight-of-hand was good, but probably nothing special. The props were appropriately dramatic. A more critical scrutiny of his offering or even a little common sense might have raised my level of suspicion, but the *sound* that soldier could produce when supposedly munching the broken glass was all the proof I needed! Of course it wasn't shards of glass being crushed between his teeth, *but it sounded like it!* And that sound was fully persuasive to my thoroughly conditioned and eagerly expectant ears. It was a lesson in communication that would take me the better part of a lifetime to assimilate.

* * *

. . . there is a music wherever there is a harmony, order or proportion; and thus far we may maintain the music of the spheres; for those well ordered motions, and regular paces, though they give no sound unto the ear, yet to the understanding they strike a note most full of harmony.

Sir Thomas Browne (1605-1682), *Religio Medici* (1643), pt.ii, 9

Jesus became the quintessential prophet, teacher and sage in part because of his unique grasp and application of a concept known as typology, from the Greek *typos*, meaning model or pattern. Nested within his remarkable aptitude was the capacity to see in the ancient Hebrew record so clear a picture and to have been so assured of its reliability that he could follow it like a map by which he plotted his course and committed himself to a certain future. The theory holds Jesus understood this, not because he was God, but because he could read the map.

With the messianic trace laid out before him and once committed to the mission, Jesus had not to search around for what to do or when and how to begin. From the salutary events at Bethany-beyond-the-Jordan to the horror of the execution outside the gates of Jerusalem, he ordered his three-and-one-half-year, one-thousand-two-hundred-sixty day mission as one seeing it spread out on a table before him. And he provided those closest to him with a clue revealing just how he knew it, frequently confirming his elected path with a succinct ". . . it is written."[6]

If one has doubt regarding the existence and reliability of historical social cycles, the theory suggests Jesus didn't. The wisdom he demonstrated consisted of a ready and accurate perception of analogies. By his actions and his words, he revealed the secret of modern prophecy – not one of burning bushes and mysterious voices, but the explanation of present and foretelling of significant future events through the understanding of cycles, i.e., types and antitypes revealed through the ancient record.

* * *

It had been almost a year since I had first presented clinical symptoms. Non-specific symptoms had presented eighteen months earlier. After months of increasingly troublesome episodes best described as compulsive behavior, I'd been awakened in the night by the distinct sensation a small insect was crawling from my nose. In the harsh, intrusive glare of the bedside lamp, the startling smear of bright red blood across the back of my hand should've raised some measure of suspicion in my hireling caretakers, but it didn't.

After passing an all-day physical examination at the county hospital, my primary care physician examined the innocuous results and concluded that I showed the full range of symptoms endemic to a widely recognized, contemporary condition known as "executive burnout." He referred me to a psychiatrist, dismissing the worrisome, now recurring nosebleed. That nosebleed, that simple yet most significant manifestation, was to be continually dismissed by the medical experts in my hire when it was, in fact, a critical symptom pointing directly to the improbable, but not inconceivable condition that was silently, insidiously choking off my life.

After dumping the full range of antidepressive and antianxiety drugs upon my already damaged physique, this psychiatrist agreed with me and concluded I didn't need a psychiatrist. He returned my case accordingly to the custody of my primary care physician. In this manner, I was sent back to the beginning on three separate occasions during my increasingly desperate search for a medical explanation of my mounting physical, mental and emotional distress.

***

What song the Syrens sang, or what name Achilles assumed when he hid himself among women, though puzzling questions, are not beyond all conjecture.
Sir Thomas Browne (1605-1682) *Urn Burial* (1658), ch.5

Ratiocination is the process of critical thinking or just a reasoned train of thought. For example, following the birth of Jesus, Mary's purification sacrifice, required by the Law of Moses, was two small birds, the minimum sanctioned offering under these circumstances, reserved for those of the most humble resources. We may thus reason that Mary and Joseph couldn't afford to purchase one of the many lambs that grazed on the Judean hills, for under the Law such a purchase and offering would have been expected of those with means.

About this same time, a company of wise men, magi who had traveled far to locate a newborn infant designated by a spectacular celestial phenomenon, opened their treasures and gave to the newborn child costly gifts of gold, frankincense and myrrh. There's no evidence Mary and Joseph ever expropriated the gifts of the magi for their necessary expenses. To the contrary, there is considerable evidence the treasure of the magi was held for the direct benefit of the child alone. It identifies the mysterious source of his sustenance during his three-and-one-half-year mission that began about thirty years later. It may also provide explanation for his abundant knowledge and fluency in the ancient Hebrew record.

Education in the Mosaic Law was not unknown among the Jews of Galilee, but Jesus was obviously educated beyond what was typical for a son of an artisan poor enough to have his wife qualify for the minimum purification offering. Although well-versed in the ancient record, Mary is an unlikely source of this fluency, for even his own townspeople, who knew Mary, questioned the source of his knowledge.

> **"Where did this man get this wisdom . . . Is this not the carpenter's son? Is not His mother called, Mary. ."**
> Matthew 13:54-55 (NASB)

His impressive, specialized knowledge of the Law – and that by the age of twelve – reflects the tutoring of a master of the Law.

The temptation has always been to jump to the conclusion that the knowledge and fluency which Jesus possessed was the divine gift of a sovereign God, in keeping with the confusing divinity of Jesus, but this needn't be so. In fact, it would be completely out of character. To understand this requires looking back to an earlier cycle, to an earlier type of the Messiah.

It's evident that sometime in the latter half of the second millennium B.C.E., after hearing the anguished cry of the Israelites who labored as slaves under their Egyptian overlords, God raised up a deliverer of those people – Moses. Extraordinary parallels exist between the lives of Moses and Jesus – some obvious (both were threatened in infancy by a royal edict calling for a slaughter of the innocent), some not so obvious (both terminated their corporal journey having only glimpsed their crowning achievement from afar). These parallels tell any who are aware they are looking at a map that Jesus came as the antitype of Moses. It was part of the sign, the signature of Messiah. Of necessity, he would be (1) born of humble parentage and (2) educated in the courts of ecclesiastical royalty. Upon (3) attaining maturity and cognizant of injustices perpetrated against the people at the hands of a privileged sacerdotal set, he would (4) distance himself from their courts immediately prior to (5) a lengthy wilderness experience, and all of this in preparation for (6) the ultimate deliverance of those same oppressed people. It all fits.

Moses was properly prepared and tested by both royal and wilderness experience, fit for duty as king or servant – or better yet, as king and servant. The Messiah would be similarly qualified. The cycle prophesied it.

. . . nothing worth proving can be proven,
Nor yet disproven: wherefore thou be wise,
Cleave ever to the sunnier side of doubt.
Alfred, Lord Tennyson (1809-1892) *The Ancient Sage* (1885), l.66

With the awareness of natural and social cycles in the ancient Hebrew record, ratiocination becomes a valid tool. It is, perhaps, even an intended tool. Its reliability must be weighed in terms of subjective probability, but on occasion that probability can be quite high. And after all, it's a process not dissimilar to that which has resulted in the morphogenesis of all the variously accepted ecclesiastical theories since the Council of Nicaea, the doctrinal congress presided over by the august Roman Emperor Constantine.

* * *

The family spent the winter of 1944-45 in Seattle. I remember the incessant rain. In the spring, we left Seattle to follow Chester to his second and last naval station at Oakland.

Oakland in the spring was a stark contrast to Seattle in the winter. Where before there had been continuous rain and cloud cover, the San Francisco Bay Area countryside was awash in sunlight and color, the striking reddish-orange and black tiger lilies lining the ditches on both sides of the country road that led to our rural boarding house.

Chester Eakins escaped overseas duty and possibly his own death that spring by a simple twist of fate. He was pulled off his departing ship at the last moment for necessary dental work. That LST was promptly sunk off the Aleutians with significant loss of life. A seventh son, he would always be surrounded by the aura of luck.

* * *

Joseph and Mary were a day's journey out from Jerusalem when they noticed their eldest son's absence. It must've taken them another day's journey to go back. After perhaps three days (by Jewish reckoning), Joseph and Mary went to the Temple where they found Jesus discoursing with the masters of the Law.

At the age of twelve, Jesus would not yet have been accorded the privileges of manhood, and it's highly unlikely the distinguished scholars and teachers of the Law routinely admitted Galilean youths of artisan parentage to their inner circle. How was it that Jesus was able to enter the vaunted Temple grounds and take a place among that princely body? Josephus, the noted first-century Jewish historian, entered into such discussions as a youth, but he was slightly – yet significantly – older at the time and born of priestly and royal blood. The theory holds Jesus was introduced – recommended, if you will – by someone known to the Temple scholars, likely one of their own, one who had been or currently was a hired tutor for the boy, compensated from the treasures of the magi.

According to Josephus' account, over a million pilgrims populated Jerusalem during the days of the Passover Feast. No doubt many had departed just as had Mary and Joseph and those with whom they were traveling, but some would have tarried. And Jerusalem was no small hamlet like Bethlehem. The Temple had twenty-thousand servants and eighteen-thousand workmen on the payroll. Joseph and Mary could not have found one boy so quickly upon returning to Jerusalem had they not known where his tutor would be found.

Since the people of Jesus' hometown thought he was unlearned, it appears Jesus was sent to Jerusalem for this tutelage, which would coincide with known custom. But, following God's instruction to the prophet Ezekiel and the typal story of the prophet Samuel, the maturing Jesus held his knowledge in secret from his local community until signaled to begin his brief, but remarkable mission by the accession of John the Baptist and a divine visitation at the waters of Bethany-beyond-the-Jordan.

It's intriguing to speculate the Jewish master may have been the eminent Gamaliel. Such intimate acquaintance may have prompted Gamaliel's wise and generous attitude toward the followers of Jesus immediately following the crucifixion.[7] Saul of Tarsus, later known as Paul, confessed he'd been a student of Gamaliel.[8] Jesus and Saul, known contemporaries, might even have had casual contact as students – Jesus of Nazareth, the clear-eyed, soft-spoken son of an obscure Galilean artisan and Saul of Tarsus, the pharisaic firebrand born to Roman citizenship.

* * *

The wall clock in the entrance foyer began to chime and continued for nine strokes, disturbing my reverie. Only at such moments was I remotely aware of time. Normally I would have no concern, but that morning was different. That morning time was of the essence. That morning, I was going to have to respond to the movement of that clock.

* * *

What if earth
Be but the shadow of Heaven, and things therein
Each to other like, more than on earth is thought?
John Milton (1608-1674) *Paradise Lost* (1667), 1668 ed. bk.v, l.574

In the ancient Hebrew record, Jonah is the prophet swallowed by the great fish in Sunday school stories. He was called by God to arise and go to Nineveh, the wicked capital city of Assyria that would eventually repent at his urging. Nineveh was a great city "three days' walk" – about sixty miles – from Jonah's hometown. Jesus was from Nazareth, an otherwise insignificant town also located in the territory of Zebulun. Nazareth was about sixty miles – a "three days' walk" – from Jerusalem.

Jonah didn't go to Nineveh immediately upon receiving his commission from God. Instead he fled by the tumultuous sea from the presence of the Lord, intending to go to Tarshish, a city long associated with wealth, power and pride. The path to Tarshish took Jonah in a direction opposite that of the road to Nineveh. It was the same option by which Satan is said to have tempted Jesus.

The storm at sea, the sleeping of Jonah during the maelstrom and the desperate pleading of the crew for his arousal and intervention are all events echoed in the accounts of the life of Jesus. But the most significant typal event is the three days and nights in the belly of the great fish. Jesus made the direct connection:

> **". . . just as Jonah was three days and three nights in the belly of the [fish], so shall the son of man be three days and three nights in the heart of the earth."** Matthew 12:40 (KJV)

The story is familiar enough. The Lord commanded the fish and it vomited Jonah up onto the dry land. Jonah arose from there and went to Nineveh. Nineveh is said to have repented at the revivified Jonah's proclamations. And when God saw by their deeds that they had turned from their ways, he relented concerning the calamity which he had declared he would bring upon them. He didn't do it. Thus, the grand design for Messiah had its perfect progenitor.

Of Jerusalem, the seat of established religiosity, Jesus said,

> **"The men of Nineveh will rise in the judgment . . . and condemn it, because they repented at the preaching of Jonah. . . ."**
> Matthew 12:41 (KJV)

The theory holds everything in the ancient record means something. If a part of Jonah's experience – the three days and nights in the belly of the fish – was a foreshadowing of the death, burial and resurrection of Jesus, as he claimed, then other characteristics of the story also provide a glimpse into the life of the Messiah. Jesus knew of the dismal temporal and splendid spiritual outcomes of his life and messianic mission because he read about and understood the messianic progenitors, including – but not limited to – Moses, Jonah, Ezekiel, Samuel, and Job. If one chooses, he can see no less than the mental and spiritual struggles of Jesus depicted in these accounts.

Jesus acknowledged the connection. Simon Barjona[9] ("son of Jonah") was not the son of an otherwise unknown first-century father named Jonah. The record never gives the name of Simon Peter's father. When Jesus referred to Simon Peter as "Simon Barjona," he was indicating Simon Peter was *his* son, *his* protégé, in the same sense that the apostle Paul later considered Timothy a son. Jesus understood that he and the prophet Jonah were, in a special sense, one and the same, type and antitype. In referring to Simon Peter as "Simon Barjona," he again revealed to Peter and the others the existence of the map and the messianic trace.

* * *

Born and raised in the church and a student of the ancient record all my life, one might have thought my Christian conviction responsible for the periodic absence of fear and anxiety, but it was the condition that was responsible for that phenomenon, not knowledge of God. Despite my decades of application, I didn't then know enough to realize my ignorance. My credentials had failed me, and I wouldn't even know it until after I should've died.

CHAPTER 3

THE LOVELY WAY

Many things I thought of then, Battle, and the loves of men,
Cities entered, oceans crossed, Knowledge gained and virtue lost,
Careless folly done and said, And the lovely way that led
To the slimepit and the mire And the everlasting fire.
A. E. Housman (1859-1936) *Last Poems* (1922), 31. *Hell Gate*

The path by which I became a partaker and guardian of the theory may have taken a lifetime, but its materialization hit me like a lightning bolt. The universal perplexity and generic demoralization that result when senseless tragedy and hardship overtake good people aren't fallout from a lack of answers in the one place where they're most expected. The answers we seek are not undecipherable. They are simply unperceived.

To reason correctly from a false premise is the perfection of sophistry. Like a window curtain, sophistry may be ornamental, but its practical effect is to keep out light. The theory suggests we have consistently failed to recognize answers because we continue to take specific venerable propositions as an indisputable starting point and never think of bringing these underlying assumptions into question. In this case, our feelings of helplessness are rooted in the false premise characteristic of all previous explicative efforts – namely, bad things happen to good people.

With effrontery uncharacteristic of a modern Christian upbringing, I weighed in my mind a heresy of the strain which had resulted in the martyrdom of early reformers going back beyond the Reformation and Jesus of Nazareth to Zechariah, son of Barachiah.[10] I considered a supposition that, until that moment, had been unthinkable. Was it conceivable lay intuition had been right all along? For those believing the Old and New Testaments to be written indirectly by the hand of God, didn't the essence of that record render the phenomenon – namely, bad things happening to good people – an anomaly of major proportions which, assurances of the clergy notwithstanding, defied rational explanation? Was it conceivable those entrusted with the keys to the mystery since at least the early-fourth-century had been – and were to the present day – mistaken? all of them? for over sixteen-hundred years?

Stung by the splendor of a sudden thought.
Robert Browning (1812-1889) *A Death in the Desert*, 1.59

In that instant, by the same stroke, it appeared not only conceivable, but probable, for in submitting the varied testimony of the ancients to the mold of this portentous conclusion, nothing bent or broke. In fact, tension throughout the entire unit relaxed, as though the flex had always been in the modern interpretation. The supposed heresy only returned the unit to a steady state. And, after all, such an astonishing ecclesiastical phase is prophesied in the record, not only by recognizable cycles, but directly by the apostle Paul in the second half of the first-century.

> **. . . be not soon shaken in mind or be troubled . . . as that the day of Christ is at hand . . . for that day shall not come, except there come a falling away first. . . .** 2 Thessalonians 2:2-3a (KJV)

Once given liberty to flow, answers that had long eluded me fairly cascaded over the top of a clerically buttressed wall that had impeded my understanding for decades. Bewildered, shell shocked, and struggling to make sense of the world I encountered daily, I realized lay intuition had been right all along. The resident experts had been – and are to this day – mistaken. Just as the priests and rulers at the mock trial of Jesus of Nazareth, they had consistently failed to recognize the answer to their forceful question when looking right at it. Those passing judgment on Jesus that dreadful night were actually part of the process of his confirmation. They were receiving the answer to their pointed inquiry . . .

> **"If You are the Christ, tell us plainly."** John 10:24 (NASB)

. . . in what they were seeing, hearing, feeling and, most especially, in what they were doing. Most simply did not see themselves in their own record. And the few that did made a cold, calculated choice.

For years I'd innately sensed something was desperately wrong. My Judeo-Christian understanding told me bad things shouldn't happen to good people . . . and they don't. For all practical purposes, there are no good people.

* * *

On the Thursday following Labor Day, 1945, Helen Eakins walked me the six blocks to Osceola's public grade school and stood me at the entrance to Mrs. James' first-grade class. I was late, very late. Not only was the morning's class well underway, but the school year had actually begun two days earlier – on Tuesday. I'd simply refused to go. But by that eventful Thursday, Helen Eakins' patience had evaporated. Welcomed as I was, I walked in with all eyes on me, interrupting the class-in-progress.

It's remarkable to me how clearly I recall the events of that day. The classroom was decorated with colorful orange and brown paper cutouts of leaves, hickory nuts, squirrels and chipmunks. The children seated around the long, low tables appeared distressingly comfortable and well-adjusted. I was awash in despair.

I accepted Mrs. James' invitation and took the only available seat, one previously assigned to another pupil who was absent that day. I was not remotely aware of the impression I must've made upon Jody Tremain.

The careful Helen Eakins, after squiring me to, from and all around the West Coast during the closing months of the war, left me there with a Roi Tan cigar box filled with the necessary minutiae. There were assorted crayons, blunt scissors so stiff they required a two-fisted grip to open and close, a sharpened pencil with a small, red plastic dime-store pencil sharpener, a sticky bottle of glue, and a dime for lunch in the school cafeteria. Never having attended day care or kindergarten, that classroom was intimidating enough for an overprotected child, but it paled in comparison with what I would experience at the morning recess. There the school yard infrastructure would emerge, the prototype for all such future encounters, born out of the commingling of power and fear, strength and weakness.

When the teacher announced recess that morning, there was a sudden flurry of activity. Dozens of little feet shuffled and small wooden chairs shrieked against the worn strip-oak flooring as children hurriedly pushed away from their tables. We'd been excused to exit in a tumultuous crowd through the empty cloakroom, into the cavernous main hallway, and out into the hot, late summer sun for thirty minutes of unstructured play.

In the long, narrow cloakroom, with naked coat hooks lining both sides of the wall and amid all the pushing and shoving, Jody Tremain grabbed me by my shoulder from behind and spun me around. Thrusting me against the wall with his forearm across my upper chest, just below the throat, he obscenely muttered something about my giving him a quarter by tomorrow or else he would beat me up. Then he was gone in the press of the other children, elbowing his way past those moving too slowly for his hurried pace.

There must have been something about the way I looked, timid and shy, or the way I stood apart from the crowd, tentative and hesitant. Whatever it was, it had been as effective as blood in the water. His rude, aggressive assault occurred so suddenly and unexpectedly, I wasn't certain I'd understood all that he said. But I understood the tone well enough. I was petrified.

As a child, I immediately understood the psychology of the angrily spoken word delivered with the authority of brute strength. I didn't appreciate it, but I understood it. It would take me decades to comprehend the threat posed by the softly spoken word delivered with the purported authority of God.

***

I have been young, and now am not too old;
And I have seen the righteous forsaken,
His health, his honour and his quality taken.
This is not what we formerly were told.

Edmund Blunden (1896-1974) *Report on Experience*

The theory holds the alarming supposition – namely, bad things *don't* happen to good people – to be entirely defensible. When skeptics reason that if Jesus was indeed Messiah and if God was indeed extant and just, then the world should be a better place – at least for good people – they do not judge altogether incorrectly. They note that active modern Christians cannot exhibit a health, wealth, or happiness profile visibly different from that of the marginally-churched, the unchurched, the never-churched, or for that matter, the totally alienated, holding lifestyle choices constant. After all, one needn't be Christian in order to live a directed, disciplined, clean, and wholesome life style. The Hasidic Jew, devout Muslim, Zen Buddhist, or humanistic atheist can do that as well, often better. Observing the absence of any real dissimilarity between the lives and fortunes of contemporary Christians vis-à-vis the thoroughly disinterested, skeptics presume the promise of a new era, the age of the mysterious kingdom of God, is a hoax perpetrated upon the desperate and/or gullible by those who would manipulate them to their own advantage. They consider the entire concept of God and the Messiah to be an indecipherable Judeo-Christian myth.

The skeptic's reasoning proceeds from the near universal assumption of a two-state universe where people are either good or bad, in or out. The theory, however, postulates an unacknowledged three-state universe consisting of (1) those genuinely in, (2) those obviously out, and (3) those widely thought to be in, but who are, in fact, out. It's the near complete vacuity of the first set and the lack of significant differences between the lives and fortunes of those in the second and third sets that fuel the skepticism.

The modern Christian, observing the same paradox with the same limited perspective, believes God exists and Jesus to be the Messiah, but the mysterious kingdom of God of which Jesus spoke (1) must be subjectively experienced or (2) is not to be experienced, as a practical matter, prior to the Second Coming. Neither the skeptic nor the modern Christian genuinely expects a visible, objective manifestation of the New Testament kingdom of God on earth for the perfectly splendid reason that they've neither experienced it nor seen it, claims to the contrary notwithstanding.

And hast thou sworn, on ev'ry slight pretence,
Till perjuries are common as bad pence,

While thousands, careless of the damning sin,
Kiss the book's outside who ne'er look within.
William Cowper (1731-1800) *Expostulation*, l.386

The contestations of both believer and disbeliever are necessary because the modern model of the Church has never achieved the extraordinary status described in the record and, as inferred by the apostle Paul, actually expected of early Christian communities. There exists instead this highly visible class of people who are *relatively* good compared to those around them and are, therefore, immediately christened – explicitly or implicitly – the "good" people. These are socially and culturally approved, law-abiding citizens living by their own good Judeo-Christian consciences. They're often, although not always, active in church attendance and civic affairs. They work hard and love their kids, exhibiting a "good" defined by contemporary standards – and most especially by contemporary ecclesiastical standards. And they are residents, by misunderstanding, of a land where exemption from misfortune is found, if at all, with dismaying inconsistency. Although naïvely anticipating such exemption, they – relatively good though they may be – are, in fact, taking their chances with the rest of the community-at-large, including the not-so-good, the bad, and the downright evil.

Of these relatively good individuals, Jesus spoke an axiom actually expounded earlier in the ancient record. It describes the predicament of the community-at-large, populated as it is by the relatively good and the obviously bad.

> **"...he maketh his sun to rise on the evil and on the good and sendeth rain on the just and on the unjust."**
> Matthew 5:45b (KJV)

And this is exactly what both the skeptic and the modern Christian observe.

In accepting the socially, culturally, and ecclesiastically defined mores of a modern society and groping therein toward knowledge of a supremely ancient, unchanging God, the theory suggests the modern Christian unwittingly bends the testimony of the ancient record whenever and wherever necessary to interface with time-warped ecclesiastical concepts. This I'd done throughout my entire Christian life . . . and I was baffled by what I perceived to be the absence of God.

*

What had always been there, operative upon me and those both before and currently surrounding me, was an analogous equivalent to natural law. In the natural world, honest misunderstanding is visited as sharply as passive indifference or willful disregard. Nature delivers the blow without a word. It's left for the wounded to figure out the explanation for the blow. For example, gravity doesn't care whether one believes in it or not. Gravity asks neither understanding nor acknowledgement. Express ignorance, disdain, disbelief, or contempt for the law of gravity, step out of a second-story window, and a moment later a rude affirmation arrives. Although its basis is abstruse, the operative effect of gravity is simple to understand and thoroughly dependable. In my case, the ground had repeatedly rushed up to challenge my decades-old effort to take wing in modern Christian air space with only a contemporary understanding of the ancient record.

Those encounters with the operative effect of this mysterious gravity hurt. Occasionally they hurt badly. Throughout all of this, I – having endeavored to live by the standards set by the relatively good people before me and currently surrounding me – struggled to comprehend the justification for the unexpected and disappointing results. There was a *transcendental* gravity defeating me at every turn, leaving me confused and bedeviled, because I lacked the understanding which consistently predicted the observed effect.

I'd spent the better part of a lifetime struggling to make sense of the world I observed and experienced daily. I was often disappointed, occasionally angry and resentful toward God, racked by alternating highs and lows in my parochial endeavor, by occasionally ecstatic feelings of confidence and worrisomely frequent sensations of chilling isolation, and all the while I was deferentially assuaged by what I still believe to be a largely well-intentioned clergy with assurances of the normalcy of the unreasonableness I both saw and felt. Affirmations that God was in his Holy Temple and that the universe was unfolding as it should left me feeling cold, empty and alone. And that's exactly what I was.

* * *

Jody Tremain was a holdover from last year's first-grade class and the undisputed first-grade school yard overlord. It's amazing to me now that one of life's most dependable truisms should be demonstrated so abruptly in my initial societal experience. There would always be a school yard overlord. In every season, in every gathering, there would always be a Jody Tremain.

At the time, I was small for my age, skinny and slight of build. With a July birthday, fully three-fourths of the students in that class were older and all the boys (as I recall) were bigger than me. Because of the school board's quaint policy of failing those students whose academic performance was less than satisfactory, some – including Jody Tremain – were much bigger. One kid was taller than the teacher.

Jody Tremain was only slightly taller than me, but much larger, more stocky than fat, built like an M4 Sherman tank with the solid stance produced by a low center of gravity. Even in that late summer heat, he wore a scarred, brown leather Army Air Corps flight jacket. One of his legs was slightly shorter than the other, and thus he both walked and ran with a permanent limp. Not at all compromising his speed and agility, the limp transformed his rapid approach and retreat into that of some grotesque miscreant.

The bully attracted a squadron of sycophants. These were lesser individuals, not bullies themselves, but individuals who became something different in the immediate presence of a Jody Tremain. Visible fear will invite danger. Like a stray dog pack, closet cowards will descend upon known ones. As surely as a Jody Tremain would always arise out of the primordial elements present in the school yard that morning, so also would this servile contingent of fawners and flatterers.

Stepping out onto the school yard, blinking in the morning sun, I stood back watching as the girls and boys separated. The girls went off to the eastern edge of the school yard to play under the numerous mature shade trees which lined that side of the square city block that was the grounds of Osceola's only elementary school. The boys, sweaty and dirty, clustered in the dusty, open area near the playground apparatus northwest of the main entrance to the school. I stood back and, rather than rushing to compete for the nearby playground equipment as did the other boys, hid behind the dense shrubbery that closely guarded the north face of the massive school building.

* * *

There's a striking confrontation between God and the relatively good of the Israelites in the ancient record. This segment – a scathing rebuke by God of his own people – is excerpted from the record according to the prophet Amos:

> **"Come to Bethel, and transgress; at Gilgal multiply transgression; and bring your sacrifices every morning, and your tithes . . . offer a sacrifice of thanksgiving with leaven and proclaim and publish the free offerings: for this liketh you, O ye children of Israel,"**

saith the Lord GOD.

> **". . . I have given you . . . [famine] in all your places . . . I have withholden rain from you . . . [and] caused it to rain upon one city, and . . . not to rain upon another . . . I have smitten you with blasting and mildew: when your gardens and your vineyards and your fig trees and your olive trees increased, the palmerworm devoured them . . . I have sent among you the pestilence after the manner of Egypt: your young men have I slain with the sword. . . . I have overthrown some of you, as God overthrew Sodom and Gomorrah . . . yet have ye not returned unto me,". . . .**
>
> Amos 4:4-10 (KJV)

The remarkable feature of this account is that these weren't the bad people of their society. Their acknowledged credits include (1) daily sacrifice at the designated temple, (2) tithing, (3) a thank offering (although not from their need, but from their abundance), and (4) highly visible free offerings. And none of this grudgingly, but with a willing, perhaps even a cheerful heart. And yet bad things were happening to *some* of them, despite their self-defined good standing. The explanation has to do with perspective or perhaps a lack thereof . . .

. . . if thou say in thine heart,

> **"Wherefore come these things upon me?"**

For the greatness of thine iniquity. Jeremiah 13:22a (KJV)

And what was the iniquity of these in the prophet Amos' account? If I maintained that chaotic circumstance randomly fell upon these people because they were engaged in idol worship, I was brought back to the beginning. There was little then to explain why, with roughly the same frequency as the visibly alienated, chaotic circumstance afflicts the congregation whose modern temples and stylized oblations are supposedly free from idol worship.

The theory acknowledges modern Christianity may have reached a level of sophistication that precludes the worship of statues of humankind and four-footed animals, but it doesn't necessarily follow that such sophistication has eliminated man's predilection for idolatry. Perhaps modern idols and their images have also become more sophisticated.

***

The female teachers were on the school yard during recess, but they stood together in the shade on the east side of the imposing north face of the school building, arms folded across their chests, talking with each other. Playground accidents and actual fighting would bring them onto the school yard, but threats and intimidation were either difficult to identify from a distance or else were considered a harmless element of playground activity.

I huddled behind the thick, mature shrubbery encircling the old three-story, redbrick schoolhouse, keenly aware of the pounding in my chest and in my ears. My head felt swollen a half-size from the pain that originated from behind the bridge of my nose. I was perspiring profusely, the sweat and dirt from the back of my hand stinging my eyes. A large flying insect buzzed by my ear, causing me to panic and furiously flay the air around my head. I thought it was a yellow jacket, but then I always thought that. I had no idea whether I was safe in the bushes. The thought hadn't consciously crossed my mind. I was reacting instinctively with the disjointed, confused mentality of some frenzied prey.

Through the leaves of the bushes, I could see the predator standing in the early September sun which still scorched the small, rural Mississippi River Delta community. Overwhelmed by my circumstance, I waited to react rather than act.

One of Jody's spaniels passed close by, saw me hiding in the bushes, and began shouting to the others. In a heartbeat, fully half of the boys in the class were rushing to where I huddled under the bushes, led by Jody Tremain with that monstrous gait. The bully ducked under the canopy of shrubbery and stalked into the shady, cleared space where I squatted, hunched down next to the massive north wall. Several of his entourage crowded into the narrow confines with him. Soiling my shirt with his dirty hands, Jody Tremain pulled me to my feet and held me firmly out in front of him. With twisted face and neck glistening with beads of dirty sweat, he made himself perfectly clear. Tomorrow! Tomorrow I'd better bring him a quarter or else he was going to beat me up.

Shoving me back against the schoolhouse wall, Jody and his entourage trooped back out into the sun and resumed their interest in the playground apparatus. I remained in the shadow of the immense school building, still partially concealed by the shrubbery, choking on fear and humiliation.

* * *

The theory holds there is another class of good people defined in the record of the ancients. This good is defined by a different standard than that used to reckon the relatively good. To those desirous of knowing more about this good, Jesus said,

> **". . . if ye love them which love you, what reward have ye . . . and if ye salute your brethren only, what do ye more than others? Do not even the publicans so?"** Matthew 5:46-48 (KJV)

Jesus suggested there was a more complete, fully-matured good that existed beyond the relative goodness of those who loved only those who loved them and those who welcomed only their own kind. He identified the Father, and indirectly himself, as the epitome of that good.

Whatever the substance of this intrinsic good of which Jesus spoke, it was clearly something beyond the socially, culturally, and ecclesiastically defined standard of the day. Of persons embodying this intrinsic good, Jesus had spoken words I'd found frustrating and bewildering for years:

> **"Ask, and it shall be given you; seek, and ye shall find; knock, and it shall be opened unto you . . ."** Matthew 7:7 (KJV)

". . . whatsoever ye shall ask in my name, that will I do . . . If ye shall ask any thing in my name, I will do it." John 14:13a,14 (KJV)

To ask in the name of Jesus did not signify some ritualistic incantation which would summon the genie from the bottle. To ask in the name of Jesus signified a petitioning with the already-ingested, fully-assimilated spirit of the man called Jesus. Therein lay the potential of the glittering promise of the New Testament kingdom of God.

The theory holds the promise was never given to the relatively good, however sincere they may be, but to those who had *already* imbibed the essence of what he was. Becoming like him in their inner-most being, these renounced, as he did, not so much privilege as all *claim* to privilege, choosing instead citizenship in the kingdom of God. Short of this, all remain vulnerable to the capricious whims of fate that afflict the community-at-large.

Of the latter day scarcity of this class of intrinsically good people, Jesus delivered a sobering prophecy. Confirming God's speedy response in bringing justice to his elect, Jesus prophesied concerning the Second Coming of the Messiah . . .

". . . when the Son of man cometh, shall he find faith on the earth?" Luke 18:8b (KJV)

. . . echoing the sentiments of the psalmist, who in an earlier cycle had remarked,

Help, LORD, for the godly man ceases! For the faithful dis-appear from among the sons of men. Psalms 12:11 (NASB)

Jesus prophesied that at or near the time of the Second Coming, these intrinsically good people would be so few it would appear as though there were none at all, the entire class having become ostensibly non-existent, just as had occurred by the early-first-century. In such an environment, sincere and well-meaning individuals, scorched by great heat, are forced to attempt awkward explanations for why bad things happen to good people, the relatively good being the only such class of people they observe.

* * *

My father never addressed the issue of the quarter I requested to buy off Jody Tremain, but that wasn't the really bad part. The really bad part came when he laughed heartily upon hearing my quivering testimony of the dramatic encounter, even calling in my visiting Aunt Lois and Uncle Arthur to join in the amusement, which they did.

In the days that followed, Jody Tremain was as threatening and intimidating as ever, constantly inflicting psychological injury on me and, I presume, others. But he never beat me up. And he never again mentioned the quarter. I actually think he forgot about it.

In retrospect, I don't think Jody Tremain took himself – what he was, what he said, or what he did – that seriously. Only I did that. With the maturity that came with the years, I acquired a qualified appreciation of that characteristic in Jody Tremain which at first I found most intimidating. He, like my father, was at least an up-front guy. He never put me on. He left no doubt concerning the nature of his intentions or his absence of sympathy for me or my circumstances. I learned to anticipate his action and reaction because he hid nothing of what he was. There was clarity about that kind of relationship. I've not missed the intimidation and humiliation, but I have indeed missed the clarity.

* * *

To live a life half dead, a living death.

John Milton (1608-1674) *Samson Agonistes* (1671), l.100

Just as there are two distinct classes of "good people" found in the ancient record, so also there are two distinct sets of "bad things." Addressing the circumstantial, senseless, often tragic bad happening, Jesus spoke on one occasion to some who were disturbed by twin tragedies that had recently visited their countrymen. The first such happening was a stealthy mass assassination of Jewish patriots at the command of the infamous Roman procurator of Judea, Pontius Pilate. The second was a deadly building collapse, a disaster that – given the presumably embryonic state of liability litigation at the time – may have left no one obviously to blame.

Because life in the community-at-large, outside the protectorate of the kingdom of God, was referred to by the ancients as "death," the people "perished" in the random occurrence of fortune and misfortune. Here's the text:

> **There were present . . . some that told him of the Galilæans, whose blood Pilate had mingled with their sacrifices. . . . Jesus answering said unto them,**
>
> > **"Suppose ye that these Galilæans were sinners above all . . . because they suffered such things? I tell you, nay: but, except ye repent, ye shall all likewise perish. Or those eighteen, upon whom the tower in Siloam fell, and slew them, think ye that they were sinners above all men that dwelt in Jerusalem? I tell you, nay: but, except ye repent, ye shall all likewise perish."**
> >
> > Luke 13:1-5 (KJV)

Just as modern man would be doing nearly two-thousand years later, first-century Israelites, ostensibly God's people, assumed they either were or should be operating within some sphere of protection from random misfortune. Even the pagan Maltese islanders believed they were protected from harm by their gods, living within a realm where misadventure happened only to people who were bad.

> **. . . when the barbarians saw the venomous beast hang on [Paul's] hand, they said among themselves,**
>
> > **"No doubt this man is a murderer, whom, though he hath escaped the sea, yet vengeance suffereth not to live."** Acts 28:4 (KJV)

The logical extension of this suggests that exemption from misfortune was anticipated for people who were good. It is to this day an axiom intrinsic to the worship of any deity. In the case of the Hebrew God, this is with ample justification. Echoes of the pronunciations of Deuteronomy 28 fairly reverberate throughout the ancient record.

> **. . . it shall come to pass, if thou shalt hearken diligently unto the voice of the LORD . . . to observe and to do all his commandments . . . that the LORD . . . will set thee on high . . . and all these blessings shall come on thee, and overtake thee. . . .**
>
> Deuteronomy 28:1-2 (KJV)

Christian doctrine of every stripe and hue, while considering its own misfortune to be a character building test of faith, has always held that those alienated from God pay a very real price for their choice. But the theory suggests that price is not necessarily a host of bad things. It is rather a life dictated by the whims of time and chance, the Shakespearean "slings and arrows of outrageous fortune."[11] The theory holds that the opposite of good isn't bad. It's chaos. And the opposite of good things isn't bad things. It's dumb luck.

Jesus wasn't the first to observe that in the community-at-large, bad things didn't necessarily happen to people because they were bad. The writings attributed to another messianic type, Solomon, a thousand years earlier addressed the unpredictable and whimsical nature of life in the community-at-large, outside the protectorate of God.

> **I . . . saw under the sun, that the race is not to the swift, nor the battle to the strong, neither yet bread to the wise, nor yet riches to men of understanding, nor yet favour to men of skill; but time and chance happeneth to them all. . . .** Ecclesiastes 9:11 (KJV)

In reaffirming what all have observed, namely, that good and bad things happen both to relatively good and relatively bad people alike, indiscriminately, Jesus implied there was another, better way. He implied there was an attainable realm immune to the capricious whims of fate. The entry thereto hinged upon a subtle quality meaning "to think differently" or "to reconsider." It's the same quality both John the Baptist and Jesus of Nazareth used to introduce the concept of the New Testament kingdom of God. Both jointly urged hearers to move from relatively good to another level of good, a giant leap beyond that of the relatively good people around them. This level of good was not attainable without imbibing the life and character of its exemplar, Jesus of Nazareth. Failing this, he prophesied all would remain vulnerable to the capricious whims of fate.

The theory holds the ethereal dimension that this subtle quality was to bring was, in fact, the mysterious New Testament kingdom of God. Not some pipedream, pie-in-the-sky, carrot-on-a-stick, pay-me-now-and-enjoy-it-later enticement as I'd been forced by circumstance to assume all my life, but the New Testament promised land in real time, where bad things don't happen to good people.

Jesus suggested this kingdom was just a step away, a step characterized by this significant quality. He said,

> **". . . except your righteousness shall exceed the righteousness of the scribes and Pharisees, ye shall in no case enter into the kingdom of heaven."** Matthew 5:20 (KJV)

The Greek word for "righteousness" meant "equity" or "innocence." According to Jesus, it wasn't the righteousness of pagans or even that of rank-and-file, backsliding believers that they had to exceed before gaining entry into the New Testament kingdom of God. It was the standard being set by the religious leadership of the day – the epitome of the relatively good people – that was responsible for their vulnerability.

However one defines that noble attribute of which Jesus spoke, the theory suggests modern Christianity has fallen short of it, its adherents exhibiting, at best, the profile of the relatively good since at least the early-fourth-century.

* * *

Welcome, thou kind deceiver!
Thou best of thieves; who, with an easy key,
Dost open life, and, unperceived by us,
Even steal us from ourselves.
John Dryden (1631-1700) *Alexander's Feast*, V. i

The lesson I took from Jody Tremain and carried with me had taken a single day to inculcate from beginning to end. But because of its subtlety, its almost universal acceptance and practice, it took me decades to understand I had less to fear from the likes of Jody Tremain than I did from my would-be spiritual guides. In time, I discovered among those presenting themselves as friend, rescuer, and pathfinder some with hidden agendum and the rest honestly – and tragically – mistaken. The former operated in the mold, but without the honesty of Jody Tremain. The latter were merely willing sycophants. It was the overlords of the contemporary Christian school yard who did, in the long run, inflict the most confusing and lasting damage.

* * *

. . . all that will live godly in Christ Jesus shall suffer persecution.
2 Timothy 3:12 (KJV)

The weave was intricate, but not inscrutable. How was it possible for one to be insulated from adversity, but simultaneously promised the same? Yet that was exactly where the ancient record had left me. Paul could and did list a veritable litany of nightmarish misfortune and this in addition to his mysterious "thorn in the flesh, the messenger of Satan."[12] Paul described himself as being "in deaths oft," again equating misfortune with the seemingly severe expression "death." He listed five times receiving forty stripes, save one; three times beaten with rods; once stoned; three times shipwrecked, and a night and a day spent in the deep. And in his frequent travels, he noted perils of dangerous river and ocean crossings, perils of robbers and the disingenuous of his number, perils from the God-fearing and the heathen, and perils in the city and in the country. He enumerated weariness and painfulness, frequent watchfulness, hunger and thirst, frequent fasting, cold and exposure. And besides these obvious hardships, he mentioned bearing the heavy mantle of responsibility for the spiritual and material welfare of his converts.[13] Yet this same Paul, following a fortnight of storm and peril on the open sea, survived together with all aboard the breakup of their ship on the rocky beaches of Malta. On that beach, he proved invulnerable to the fourth element of the feared biblical quadrumvirate of sword (war), famine (want), pestilence (disease), and wild beasts (natural disaster).

. . . when Paul had gathered a bundle of sticks, and laid them on the fire, there came a viper out of the heat, and fastened on his hand . . . . and he shook off the beast into the fire, and felt no harm. Acts 28:3-5 (KJV)

Paul, although exposed to a panorama of indisputable hardship imposed by man and nature on the one hand, was – on the other hand – surrounded by an aura of invincibility.

How can these things be? The answer lies in the recognition of a second class of "bad things."

The theory agreeably holds that in the community-at-large, some win the lottery and some are struck by lightning, a few quite literally, a great many figuratively, and this without discrimination.

However, those experiencing these capricious whims of fate are insulated from a peculiar class of hardship which visibly affected Jesus and his immediate followers, including Paul. The good news is that exemption from the random occurrences of misfortune that decimate the ranks of those in the community-at-large is available. The bad news – if indeed it is bad news – is that such individuals are virtually guaranteed the same panorama of hardship that fell upon Jesus, probably in rough proportion to their ambition, just as in the case of the apostle Paul. It's a peculiar class of hardship generated by the indignation of entrenched religiosity and, on occasion, by God to serve a divine purpose. If *ex post facto* to Christian service, as was the flogging of Peter and the others before the Council, such hardship became a badge of honor, a kind of knighthood into the Order of Jesus of Nazareth.

> **And they departed from the presence of the council, rejoicing that they were counted worthy to suffer shame for his name.**
> Acts 5:41 (KJV)

When antecedent to Christian service, such hardship became an avenue whereby the will of God was effected, as in the case of the aforementioned Maltese shipwreck.

> **. . . the chief man of the island . . . Publius . . . received us . . . and it came to pass, that the father of Publius lay sick . . . to whom Paul entered . . . and healed him. . . . when this was done, others also which had diseases in the island came and were healed. . . .** Acts 28:7-9 (KJV)

Paul and his companions were stranded on the island for three months. The ancient record doesn't tell us, but it requires no great leap of faith to surmise that by means of this apparent misadventure, the message Paul was so diligent to express among the Gentiles at every opportunity was similarly disseminated among these pagan islanders. Thus the veracity of Paul's words in his letter to the Romans, a passage circumscribing the sanctuary of those intrinsically good inhabitants of the New Testament promised land, was graphically illustrated.

> **. . . all things work together for good to them that love God. . . .**
> Romans 8:28a (KJV)

The hardships Paul endured in service to God worked for good because Paul and those to whom he addressed this axiom were residents of the New Testament kingdom of God. They were insulated against capricious, senseless hardship and tragedy, vulnerable only to that resulting directly from their commitment to God and Jesus.

The theory holds God to be far removed from responsibility for the senseless hardship and tragedy that afflicts both the relatively good and the community-at-large. That is instead a characteristic of human existence against which God, through the Messiah, has dutifully provided a sphere of protection – the New Testament kingdom of God.

The theory forced me to a difficult conclusion. If in retrospect a specific hardship or tragedy appears to have been senseless . . . it probably was.

*

They are ill discoverers that think there is no land, when they can see nothing but sea.

Francis Bacon (1561-1626) *Advancement of Learning*, II.vii.5

While the teachings of Jesus held out the promise of insulation against senseless hardship and tragedy, the dominant expressions of the post-Nicene Church – Catholic and Protestant, traditional and evangelical – have instead observed continuing misfortune. This has remained a permanent condition of life for those ostensibly Christian. Rather than view this as evidence of a failure to enter in and possess the New Testament kingdom of God, official Christendom has instead become imbued with a passive resignation. And while fortune and misfortune are indiscriminately distributed among the visibly religious and the totally alienated, the visibly religious of modern society are, for the most part, honored and praised for their high profile Christian walk, not persecuted. The theory holds resolution of the paradox lies in the conclusion that the relatively good simply are not who and what they believe themselves to be.

*

In nature there are neither rewards nor punishments – there are consequences.

Robert G. Ingersoll (1833-1899) *Lectures & Essays*

Surely it disturbs modern sensibilities to think that relatively good persons experience senseless tragedy and hardship. Surely it disturbs modern sensibilities to think that relatively good persons effectively wander in the same latter-day wilderness as the not-so-good, the bad, and the downright evil. And all this because of an honest misunderstanding and trust in a leadership that has – largely unwittingly – failed to guide them into the promised New Testament kingdom of God. All such thinking begins and ends in futility. Men groan and the souls of the wounded cry out, but God does not pay attention to folly,[14] nor does he answer to the pride of man. Transcendental gravity is simply operative, and I'd become so conditioned to the consequences of its violation, I considered it only a discouraging, perplexing facet of the Christian walk.

* * *

Sleeping fitfully, I could tell when the periodic, low-grade fever left me around midnight every night. Even while asleep, I was conscious of the blissful relief that came with its departure.

I'd awakened that September morning as the first glow of light revealed itself at the edge of the heavy drapes shrouding the windows of our bedroom. I often lay there in the stillness, listening to the steady drone of the ceiling fan, just thinking. That brief interlude between awakening and arising had become for me the clearest and purest. At that moment, in the absence of the low-grade fever, which would remain in abeyance until about noon, I could almost believe I was well again. The omnipresent fatigue was recognizable, but tolerable at that moment. It would become much more pronounced with any attempted activity, such as arising. The moment of awakening, although less-than-perfect, had become the high water mark of my day.

I could never resist the temptation to bring my right hand up and stroke it across my chest and upper abdomen, always checking to be sure if perhaps it had all been a bad dream, if perhaps I was well after all. But no, it was still there, just as it had been upon retiring the night before, an unnaturally hard mass the size of a small football beneath and slightly exuding below the rib cage on my right side.

I've never been able to understand why I didn't notice it earlier. It seemed to me as though it developed instantaneously, suddenly crystallized out of air and space following the initial variceal hemorrhage. The doctors told me it couldn't have happened that way, but why had neither Anna nor I noticed it earlier? And why had the medical tests and examinations, including the abdominal probing and poking during two extensive physical examinations in the previous eighteen months failed to detect so serious a condition? I expended much mental and emotional energy pursuing that classic example of useless, unproductive questioning, getting absolutely nowhere.

I never felt up to the task, but I had to initiate the putting together of the man every morning. It was as much a mental task as a physical one. Oh sure, I knew I could do it, but I didn't want to do it. It was as though I needed to make a conscious decision before taking each step, before every motion, no matter how mundane, no matter how routine. The medical literature labeled this most insidious of symptoms "inanition" – emptiness, lethargy, lack of vitality or vigor. It omitted the precise expression I found most descriptive – loss of spirit.

As I'd done every morning for the past few months, I put my feet over the side of the bed and sat up, only to sense the crushing weight of the fatigue. But I couldn't lie down and wait for a better moment or a better hour. It wouldn't be getting any better. From the apogee upon awakening, the less-than-perfect but nevertheless high water mark of my day, to the absolute perigee was a matter of only a few moments and perhaps six or eight shuffling steps from the bed to the bathroom mirror.

CHAPTER 4

AN UMBILICATE VULNERABILITY

There's a problem in expressing thoughts and ideas conveyed in one language in the vocabulary and syntax of another. The difficulty is compounded when translating ancient languages. If this weren't enough, the complexity of reconstructing in another dialect a source text replete with symbolism and steeped in shadow and reflection can scarcely be exaggerated. The dilemma is indigenous to the nature of languages – no translation is accomplished without the translator reading into the translation, not the words, but the *meaning* of the original communication. By this indispensable requirement, the translation of any complex material may be flawed. The process is known as *eisegesis*, the subjective reading into the text being translated an *a priori* bias.

*

Language is only the instrument of science,
and words are but the signs of ideas:
I wish . . . the instrument might be less apt to decay,
and that signs might be permanent,
like the things which they denote.
Samuel Johnson (1709-1784) *Dictionary of the English Language* (1775), preface

Words are arbitrary signposts agreed upon to describe objects and ideas. Over time, a culture gives its own meanings to words. Those of that culture hear words spoken or written in the context of their own cultural predisposition. For instance, one reading the word "church" in the New Testament doesn't comprehend the word as it was perceived by the author, but rather with the meaning with which the word is associated in the contemporary culture. In translation, the source text may lose – or gain – something not altogether insignificant.

"Never forget, gentlemen," he said, to his astonished hearers, as he held up a copy of the 'Authorized Version' of the Bible,

"never forget that this is not the Bible," then, after a moment's pause, he continued, "This, gentlemen, is only a translation of the Bible."

Richard Whately, Archbishop of Dublin (1787-1863) To a meeting of his diocesan clergy. H. Solly, *These Eighty Years* (1893), vol. II, ch. ii, p.81

As a child, I'd originally been under the impression the ancient Hebrew record had been handed down from antiquity in King James English. Common sense might have corrected that misconception, but the matter simply never came up. Clergy and laity alike considered their King James translation ordained of God. Although the original text may have been, it was a quantum leap from that to the early-seventeenth-century interpretations of a small body of individuals of whom today we know virtually nothing.

Even after becoming aware the oldest manuscripts of the record were written in ancient Hebrew (with a smattering of Aramaic) and Greek, I naïvely assumed those undertaking such a monumental task as translating the ancient record from the earliest available manuscripts set aside all presupposition when doing so. The assurance assumed to eliminate such intrusion had always been a form of collectivism. But if the ancient Hebrew record and its Greek complement are to be the measuring rod, weak assurance that is indeed.

In time, I became cautiously suspicious whenever the preacher readily vaulted to the conclusion his King James text was inspired of God, as was – or so we all believed – the Word to the ancients. Such a conclusion is a convenient supposition. It may be an attractive supposition because it ostensibly relieves the seeker of an otherwise daunting personal responsibility for his current condition. But alas, there is no such relief. Earth buries, wind parches, fire burns, and water drowns. Cause and effect are inseparable and inevitable. Natural law is just, dependable, and unrelenting. And transcendental gravity is simply operative.

* * *

I always voted at my party's call,
And I never thought of thinking for myself at all.

W. S. Gilbert (1836-1911) *H.M.S. Pinafore* (1878), I

In attempting to fulfill its evangelical commitment to the community, the little congregation of the church in Osceola arranged for an annual summer fortnight of tent meetings. Twisting around in my front row seat and clutching the back of my rented, wood-slatted, folding funeral parlor chair, I looked out over the sea of white faces, fascinated by the disparate motion of perhaps two-hundred funeral parlor fans as they flicked from every other wrist.

A small cadre of the colored also came, but they sat in rows of chairs set up alongside the tent, out from under the tent's awning. When the lengthy service was over, they didn't mingle with the milling crowd, but melted away into the darkness surrounding the cavernous, well-lighted tent.

It is piteously doleful, nodding every now and then towards dullness; well stored with pious frauds, and, like most discourses of the sort, much better calculated for the private advantage of the preacher than the edification of the hearers.
Edmund Burke (1729-1797) *Observations on a Publication, 'The present state of the nation,'* (1769)

I sat dutifully in the hard, folding funeral parlor chairs throughout the long evenings of singing and preaching, the visible perspiration on the back of my shirt and at my armpits matching that of the tireless preacher. This, of course, provided measurable testimony of just how much I was willing to suffer for the Lord.

Perhaps I had it coming for being by nature so desirous of pleasing, so trusting in what the adults told me. Perhaps I was supposed to know at that age the games people played, the deception – even the self-deception – in which they engaged. Perhaps I was a sheep waiting to be sheared, cannon fodder for the generals on the hill, one of those born every minute that made P. T. Barnum a rich man, or just the most elemental component of the food chain. But whatever, I swallowed whole that which was so emphatically put before me without savoring so much as a morsel.

* * *

It's not just what we inherit from our mothers and fathers that haunts us. It's all kinds of old defunct theories, all sorts of old defunct beliefs. It's not that they actually live on in us; they are simply lodged there, and we cannot get rid of them.
Henrik Ibsen (1828-1906) *Ghosts* (1881), Act 2

None of the contemporary translations of the ancient record are free of the biases that affected the early scholars and their translated works. The bias has always been in the minds of men. Translators, both then and now, are individuals who are the product of all that has gone before them and – most assuredly – that which currently surrounds them. They are individuals who are at least subconsciously vulnerable to the same weaknesses, the same financial, social, cultural, and political nudging that influenced the work of their predecessors hundreds of years ago. The biases of the early scholars, whether freely embraced or induced by the subtle (and occasionally not-so-subtle) nudging of socio-political necessity, had to find their way into the translations they rendered. The translators couldn't remain true to their task if they did not translate the meaning, *as they understood it*, not just the words. If they were possessed of a collective bias, that bias would provide spin that was never there and forever tilt the text, becoming an integral part of the text.

The theory holds critical *a priori* bias characteristic of post-fourth-century ecclesiology is embedded in the granite substratum of the modern Christian faith. In the English case, this occurred at the time of the earliest popular translations about five-hundred years ago, and tradition, that durable god of pharisaic theism, has since fossilized those misconceptions into perpetuity.

*

Tradition means giving votes to the most obscure of all classes, our ancestors. It is the democracy of the dead . . .

G. K. Chesterton (1874-1936) *Orthodoxy* (1909), 4.The Ethics of Elfland

Centered on the European continent, the Protestant Reformation was the most widely recognized effort aimed at correcting inherent, visible abuse in ecclesiastic doctrine and practice. Martin Luther and other reformers of the late-fifteenth- and sixteenth-centuries were best positioned to eliminate this bias because they willingly placed themselves outside the loop, enduring excommunication and martyr-dom, even as Jesus had done fifteen-hundred years earlier. Had these late-fifteenth- and sixteenth-century reformers and their followers been free of bias regarding a specific characteristic of the Church, the Reformation might have restored the simplicity so vitally important to first-century Christianity, but reformers can't eliminate bias they themselves possess. Neither can translations that are a product of and/or dependent on an entrenched ecclesiology. There's simply too much at stake.

Once fixed in the English translations of the ancient record, this bias left the domain of the scholar. With the increasing literacy of the common man, it permeated the laity, reinforcing the iron yoke that for each successive generation has been largely responsible for the disillusioning failure to lay hold of the promises of God expounded from Moses to Jesus. But all this must unfold as it should.

* * *

We were, fair queen,
Two lads that thought there was no more behind
But such a day tomorrow as today,
And to be boy eternal.
We were as twinn'd lambs that did frisk i' the sun,
And bleat the one at the other: what we chang'd
Was innocence for innocence; we knew not
The doctrine of ill-doing, no, nor dream'd
That any did.

William Shakespeare (1564-1616) *The Winter's Tale*, I.ii.62

In the placid ambience of small town existence in the rural Mid-South of the late '40s, Dwayne Lee Penry and I forged the bonds of friendship. Dwayne and I were first cousins. I was two years older, but by early adulthood, Dwayne and I – by virtue of the physical stature, personality and temperament we each inherited from the venerable Elijah Roy – could've been brothers, even twins.

With summer sweat dripping from our faces, Dwayne and I rushed through Helen Eakins' screened back porch door and sprawled on the living room floor before a large black, incredibly heavy Hunter table fan. We delighted in the cool rush of the wind passing across our wet faces, rippling our damp shirts. We'd speak silly phrases and make long, extended "ahhhhh" sounds into the electric fan, ecstatic at hearing the whirring blades chop the sound into a staccato rhythm.

Without the distractions of television, Dwayne and I gamboled across the front lawn in the warm twilight of those long summer evenings, chasing fireflies to incarcerate in empty fruit jars and dodging the bats which swept low over our heads. No doubt the bats were feeding on insects active at that particular time of day, but we didn't know that. We thought they were trying to get into our hair.

Our gnarled old great-grandmother, the ancient Nona Ward, had told us that story. Whether she believed it or merely delighted in the excitement it generated among her many great-grandchildren, I'm not prepared to say. We believed it because we were wide-eyed, unsuspecting children who had been informed by someone with authority, someone we assumed should know.

In retrospect, a measure of culpability rightly rested upon us. You see, it was what we wanted to believe. That fantasy was an important component in making our summer world turn. It helped fill – and pleasurably so – the long summer evening's void. Similar to the Santa Claus fantasy, it wasn't the truth – but it worked. In fact, the truth would've disappointed us. At that stage, we valued the fantasy more than the reality.

When I became a man, I realized how even a well-intentioned lie that may have had its beginnings in innocence, superstition or misunderstanding can, with time, become self-perpetuating and thoroughly addictive. When the lie has convinced us it works for us, we no longer have the motivation to seek truth. And if we stumble across truth at all, it's unexpected and threatening to our sense of order. At that point, we've become no longer pilgrims, but landlords, no longer seekers of an elusive truth, but defenders of a decidedly material privilege. As when first confronted with the truth regarding the Santa Claus fantasy, we may angrily resist truth and in our aggrieved loss of innocence doggedly cling to the lie, emphatically affirming that it is, in fact, the truth.

It's entirely possible the arcane old woman actually believed the bat story.

* * *

Words are wise men's counters, they do but reckon by them: but they are the money of fools that value them. . . .

Thomas Hobbes (1588-1679) *Leviathan* (1651), pt.i, ch.4

If upon the initial hearing of another's name one presumed to know and understand the essence and physical appearance of that individual, the attempted description would be presumptuous and, undoubtedly, flawed. How much more my presumptive error when I accepted at face value that which was conveyed in King James English by the word "church"? There is no instance of *eisegesis* more glaring and damaging than the rendering of the Greek *ekklesia* into the English "church." Without conscious awareness, I took for granted the source of that foundational translated expression, accepting as a matter of faith the late-twentieth-century image it summoned forth. I was confident the Greek *ekklesia* was, in fact, what it was called in the English translations, whether that be (1) the body of believers, local and general; (2) a special-use parcel of real estate; (3) the clergy; or (4) the act of public worship. Thus, the rent veil of the Temple was restored by means of the subtle fabric of linguistic interpretation, for the Greek *ekklesia* carried with it none of these contemporary definitions of "church." The modern concept of Church is neither Hebraic nor early Christian. The origin of the modern model is more nearly found in ancient Canaanite and Graeco-Roman culture.

Understanding more completely the manner in which this English word evolved, the theory called me to a keen awareness of the frail position to which I'd smugly clung during my modern Christian walk. Justifying my chosen status and finding balm in the assertion that I believed in God and Jesus Christ and had elected membership in good standing in the church, I readily assumed by that binate couplet I'd satisfied some major requirement of the Most High God. But belief was never so passive nor assemblage so expurgatorial.

* * *

Elijah Roy was an enigma, even in his day, and his mystique swelled enormously in the years following his piteous demise. He was a quiet man, perhaps withdrawn, surely brooding, born and raised an orphan in west Tennessee from 1888 until 1910. After immigrating to the Missouri Bootheel, he was attempting to board a moving freight train with two companions when he misjudged its speed and was thrown beneath the wheels of the train. The following day, that same freight train made a special stop near the neighboring farm house where he lay injured all night, allowing him to be loaded on board and transported to the hospital in Memphis. His crushed left arm required amputation at the shoulder. The missing arm caused a structural imbalance that resulted in chronic back pain the rest of his life.

Trained as a telegrapher and given a job by the railroad following the accident, he married Lila Ward in 1913. He was later a businessman with two small business establishments – a grocery store and a pool hall. Grocery stores may have been benign enough, but pool halls in the early-twentieth-century could attract a rough clientele. On one occasion, he broke a cue stick over the head of an unruly customer.

He was a master at pool and could steadily align his cue stick without the aid of a bridge. This doesn't seem so remarkable for a man who at sixty years of age guided mule and moldboard plow in the withering heat of east-central Arkansas' late spring and early summer sun. He rolled his own tobacco and tied perfect loops in the laces of his scruffy brogans, all with just one hand. I personally witnessed these phenomena, the latter at close range while on my hands and knees at his feet. I could not then nor can I tell you now the mechanics of how he accomplished such a feat. His five fingers moved as swiftly as those of a master banjoist, as deftly as the striking garden spider which, working its multiple appendages with startling orchestration, wrapped its hapless victim in its marvelous autumnal web beneath my bedroom window.

* * *

We dissect nature along lines laid down by our native language. . . . Language is not simply a reporting device for experience but a defining framework for it.

Benjamin Whorf (1897-1941) *Thinking in Primitive Communities*, in Hoyer (ed.), *New Directions in the Study of Language*, 1964

Taken from two Greek words that together suggest "the called out of/from," the Greek *ekklesia* referred to any assembly of people who were called out of (or from) a larger set. The 1611 King James Version and subsequent offerings translate the word as "church" – with all its hybrid meanings – in the vast majority of its one-hundred-sixteen appearances in the New Testament.

The book of Acts contains twenty-four of those appearances of *ekklesia*, indicating the author's (Luke) familiarity with the word in a missive describing the early history of the movement identified then only as "the way." Documenting the development of the early congregations, Luke, a physician and companion of the apostle Paul, used this Greek word three times in which it simply *cannot* be translated "church." In each case, he was referring to the riotous pagan mob at Ephesus who, egged on by some who correctly perceived the messengers' teaching to be a threat to their livelihood, rushed out of the city in confusion to the theater (forum), dragging along Paul's traveling companions, Gaius and Aristarchus. In order to preserve an *a priori* concept regarding the nature and character of the Church, an inconsistent – but proper – rendering of *ekklesia* is forced in these passages. On these three occasions, the Greek *ekklesia* is translated as the generic "assembly."

The ruins of this Roman forum are still standing near the harbor at the mouth of the river Cayster. The ruins of the ancient city are five to seven miles inland. Thus, the theater which was the location of this incident was about two hour's walk from the city. This particular mob of idolatrous Ephesians was "called out (of/from)" the city to this location for a special session of the regular town meeting. Its purpose was to discuss what to do with these sojourners and their teaching which, if accepted by the people, threatened economic ruin for some who were financially dependent on the temple-based worship of the goddess Artemis (Diana).

When Luke penned the book of Acts, the neophyte Christian movement in Jerusalem had been established for some time. The educated Luke knew this, yet he showed no reluctance in referring to this pagan mob by the Greek *ekklesia*, i.e., "church" in modern usage. Luke had no reluctance to use the word in this instance because the Greek *ekklesia* did not refer to Christians or the Church as is conveniently supposed. Simply put, *ekklesia* was not a term sanctioning the modern concept of the Church, despite the fact that is the way the word is received today when reading the translated record.

* * *

Elijah Roy had been a pillar of the church in his small Missouri Bootheel farming community when by a dramatic decision he altered the course of his life. He was fifty-five years old when he simply quit and walked away.

Helen Eakins later said that he got tired of people, that he was a sensitive man and too many in whom he'd invested a portion of himself had let him down. That, however, may have been her interpretation of events she was in no position to understand. In any case, he sold nothing and took nothing with him. Leaving everything in place – home, wife, adult children and young grandchildren, his leadership in the church and his position as a city alderman – he simply walked away.

In 1943, he acquired a forty-acre wooded tract in the rugged White River Bottoms of east-central Arkansas and removed himself to that remote location. At his age and with his handicap, he set out to carve a home place from some of the wildest country then still in existence. With only one arm, dynamite, and a mule, he began to clear timber and prepare the new ground for planting cotton – the cash crop – and corn, which provided feed for the mule, the hogs, and the chickens.

Lila Roy initially remained in the Bootheel, but a few months later she joined him in that place, which although not the end of the world was surely among its last outposts.

There were neighbors, although more distant, even in the White River Bottoms. A colored man I knew only as "Buddy" had brought his young family with him to that forbidding station. Buddy and the few white inhabitants of that area worked together helping Elijah Roy, and he reciprocated, helping them in true pioneer fashion. In the rugged backwoods, where obstacles made dependence upon one another a necessity, the color barrier of the time relaxed. This colored family – Buddy, his wife and twin baby daughters – often visited in the Roy's primitive backwoods home. A few years later, this same family would join Lila and Elijah Roy in watching the grainy television made possible by the REA, Chester Eakins' generosity, and a weak television signal from Memphis.

* * *

Faith, fanatic Faith, once wedded fast
To some dear falsehood, hugs it to the last.
Thomas Moore (1779-1852) *The Veiled Prophet*, iii. l.356

"The way," as it was first called, was a movement, not an institution as it is today. Even its legitimate first-century designation, the way, meant only a road or a progressive journey. It was not an expression used exclusively to designate votaries of Jesus. Only the term "Christian" would be so specific. The evolution of *ekklesia* into its modern form, the Church, resulted from centuries of conditioning by largely pagan elements, most notably those that accompanied Roman Emperor Constantine's legitimization of Christianity in the early-fourth-century. The subsequent amalgamation of the body and the solidification of temple-based, ceremonial homage followed. By the end of the fourth-century, much of official Christianity consisted of an exterior of Judeo-Christian deference wrapped around a thoroughly pagan core.

The Roman Emperor Constantine had, perhaps unwittingly, administered the *coup de grace* that completed the eclipse of prototypal Christianity. And he did it not with sword, nor fire, nor wild beasts, but with an embrace – a kiss, if you will.

Constantine remains an enigmatic figure. He may well have been motivated by political concerns when he accepted Christianity. Then again, his acceptance may have been sincere. Scholars and authorities still debate the matter. It's possible Constantine himself may not have been able to recognize his true motive. Among the many reforms he initiated favorable to Christianity, he granted the clergy freedom from all state taxation, the equivalent of today's tax-exempt status, which had always been the privilege of priests of recognized pagan religions. The result was predictable: those seeking relief from the heavy taxation which was crushing the privileged stratum of that society began entering the Christian priesthood in such numbers that additional action was required to limit ordination.

Significantly, the house of Constantine embarked upon a policy of construction, building churches after the manner of existing pagan temples and modifying existing structures of pagan worship into such churches, all on a grand scale, and he invited Christian bishops to do likewise. The model of the legitimized Church which emerged following the Constantinian sanction of 313 is, for all practical purposes, the sole model of the modern Church.

As inferred, this model did not result entirely from Constantine's influence. There is evidence the evolution of the prototypal model of the early assembly had begun prior to the close of the first-century with the rise of the presiding bishop, the singular prelacy.

> **I wrote unto the church: but Diotrephes, who loveth to have the preeminence among them, receiveth us not. Wherefore, if I come, I will remember his deeds which he doeth, prating against us with malicious words: and not content therewith, neither doth he himself receive the brethren, and forbiddeth them that would, and casteth them out of the church.**
> 3 John 9-10 (KJV)

As early as the beginning of the second-century, secular history reveals a developing partition into clergy and laity in some assemblies. In time, the Christian priesthood developed, influenced by the officialdom that characterized the ubiquitous Roman Empire.

> **. . . The scribes and the Pharisees . . . all their works they do for to be seen of men: they . . . love the uppermost rooms at feasts, and the chief seats in the synagogues, And greetings in the markets, and to be called of men, Rabbi, Rabbi. But be not ye called Rabbi: for one is your Master, even Christ; and all ye are brethren.** Matthew 23:2,5-8 (KJV)

Ignatius, bishop of the Church in Antioch, wrote letters to several churches while on a journey to Rome early in the second-century. These letters have survived. Therein, Ignatius enjoins obedience to the singular bishop, speaks of presbyters and deacons as recognized officers in the Church, and commands that they be heeded, but he declares the singular bishop representative of God the Father. The laity may have been the Sanhedrin of God, but nothing was done without the approval of the singular bishop.

Once this early drift of the assembly's structure towards priesthood was confirmed by the Constantinian sanction, the mindset of the Church, which had already begun to recede from warm, hopeful latitudes, passed beyond its figurative Arctic Circle and became fixed in relentless ice. Nearly nineteen-hundred years later, the small fundamentalist congregation of the church in Osceola would still have its *de facto* singular prelacy. He was, of course, the resident preacher.

* * *

The White River Bottoms, Phillips County, Arkansas
Summer, 1948

Late on a Saturday night, in a remote clearing deep in the wild White River Bottoms of east-central Arkansas, Dwayne and I waited together on the open front porch of our maternal grandparents' primitive backwoods cabin. Dangling our bare legs over the rough edges of the wood-plank decking, we were careful to avoid splinters, although never completely successful. Slapping at the mosquitoes that buzzed our ears and occasionally brushed our faces, we gazed into the pitch-black darkness down the dirt road where we expected to see Chester Eakins and Elijah Roy returning from their nocturnal visit to the black-water sloughs.

Once darkness fell in the rugged backwoods where there was no electricity for radio or lights, time slowed and stagnated like the water of the innumerable borrow pits of that region. The borrow pits (locally pronounced BAR-pitz) were rectangular ponds several acres in size created by the Army Corps of Engineers when dredging material for construction of the nearby levees. These large ponds had been stocked by the State Game and Fish Commission and were teeming with bream, catfish and bass. The plentiful natural waterways were home to grinnel, carp, and gar. Both sheltered other denizens semi-aquatic – some reptilian, some amphibian, some avian.

That night, in a ritual repeated on more than one occasion during our youth, Dwayne and I awaited the return of the patriarchs of our family from the sloughs where they'd gone frog-gigging.

* * *

A Darwinian evolution has resulted in the disintegration of the once pristine, crystalline concept the apostle Peter referred to as "the way of the truth." What exists today is a swarm of fragmentary sub-models, all separate theories of the proper evolution of a remarkably successful prototype. Despite often great doctrinal differences, all these fragmentations have one undeniable characteristic in common – all are "churches" in the metamorphic post-Constantinian mold.

Supposedly, the ultimate Judeo-Christian goal has always been a single theory describing the divine order and man's purpose in it. Such a theory was the intent of both the Council of Nicaea in 325 and Martin Luther's reformation movement, most visibly initiated at Wittenberg in 1517. Ostensibly, it has been the ambition of every wind of doctrine since. I'd personally spent the best years of a modern Christian lifetime in search of that theory. But I never suspected the effort was fatally flawed from the beginning by the sophistic presumption that the solution – the ultimate theory, i.e., the "true" church – lay somewhere among the broad, expansive field of existing ecclesiastical theories or, failing that, at least within the same homogenous *class* of such theories. Following the alterative storm, I realized I had been wrong on all counts.

A noble endeavor, the exhumation and restoration of first-century Christianity, but the theory insists the issue at stake is not – at least not directly – the salvation of the soul, that bloodstained crusade that has inflamed the passions of so many for so long. According to the theory, the salvation of the soul – the driving, age-old evangelistic mission of the Church – is available within the modern Church, even as it is outside its walled citadels, among the unchurched. It's available through the Messiah, a salvation not because of the protean Church, but in spite of it, a salvation "yet so as by fire."[15] If this is the case, there may be no compelling reason for many to seek the unfamiliar essence of first-century Christianity – unless the promise of the New Testament kingdom of God in real time, that elusive fulfillment of the promises modern Christians so instinctively seek, lies just beyond that door which, for all practical purposes, has been closed for over sixteen-hundred years.

* * *

Yawning frequently, neither Dwayne nor I allowed sleep to overtake us. After staring into the pitch black darkness for what seemed to be an eternity, we spotted the twin carbide head lamps worn by Chester Eakins and Elijah Roy, dancing like suspended ghosts a quarter-mile down the dirt road which led to and terminated at the home place. Within a few minutes, the two men came out of the darkness and up to the front porch with a large burlap sack filled with perhaps two dozen large bullfrogs.

The frog legs were destined for breakfast the next morning. Tired as they were and as late as it was, Chester Eakins and Elijah Roy sat on the front porch steps and prepared those frogs by the light of two kerosene lanterns.

Since the only edible part of the frog was the hind legs, they cut the legs off and threw the remainder of the live frog out into the darkness on the dirt yard in front of the house. When they were finished, they brought the frog legs into the house to cool in a large wooden tub that sat beneath the hand pump on the screened back porch. It was then that Dwayne and I took the kerosene lanterns and stepped out into the darkness beyond the front porch.

There they were, two dozen now little frogs, all that remained of what once had been big frogs, all struggling with pitiful little motions, all trying to jump as though they still had legs. Their spirit was willing, but their magnificent propulsion units, their legs, were gone – and they didn't even know it.

By morning, every remnant of those pitiful little frogs had disappeared. If the raccoons, skunks, opossums and other nocturnal predators didn't get them, the scavenging birds and barnyard fowl did shortly after sunrise.

I can't erase the image of those legless little frogs and their pitiful little movements, trying to jump when they had not the power to do so, unaware that they weren't getting anywhere. Failing to comprehend the magnitude of the catastrophe which had befallen them, they continued on in that same futile effort. It was all they knew to do.

* * *

How often misused words generate misleading thoughts.

Herbert Spencer (1820-1903) *Principles of Ethics,* bk.I, pt.ii, ch.8, 152

The possibility of centuries-old misconception implanted in the translation of the ancient record was unsettling, but unavoidable. That misconception, once acknowledged, explained that which I hadn't been able to understand and ended the need for the weak assurances of the clergy that all was well when, quite obviously, all was not well.

My own cost had been the best years of my life and so many thousands of dollars I dared not an accounting. Not understanding all there was to understand, I acted upon that which I did understand. Letting go of what was over and done, I reached out for that which had been right in front of me all along, shrouded by my blind sight.

* * *

Physicians of the utmost fame
Were called at once, but when they came
They answered, as they took their fees,
'There is no cure for this disease.'
Hilaire Belloc (1870-1953) *Henry King*

Anna and I had known for almost a year that I was terminally ill. Until about two months earlier, we'd known only the fact and not its explanation. It's difficult to comprehend how that question swelled in significance once it became obvious I wasn't going to get well. To have one's life come to an abrupt and premature end while being deprived of knowing what had gone so desperately wrong struck me as incredulous.

A local doctor, the thirteenth physician and fourth gastroenterologist to consider my case during the eighteen-month-long diagnostic phase, had in the end grown weary of my protestations regarding the previous diagnoses, including his own. Yet he possessed enough scientific curiosity to prescribe what he referred to as "the only significant test" that had not been performed – a relatively simple venogram.

I know he didn't expect to find what he and so many others had missed. As I sat in his office the morning he made the appointment for me to once again be admitted to the local hospital, it was obvious he was not particularly enthusiastic about the procedure. He was ordering it because of my dogged refusal to accept the casual, default diagnosis all others had so readily settled upon. I was still desperately seeking a credible explanation, even if the experts were already settled upon their conclusions. I was still seeking an answer because the pain, the confusion, the living tragedy that was unfolding was *mine*.

The venogram was conducted the morning of the following day. Early that evening, this doctor fairly charged into my hospital room, ecstatic in his discovery. The first words he spoke came while he was still in full stride, exploding through the open doorway of my hospital room and circling around the foot of my bed. Although he would never again make such a positive, unqualified statement, it wouldn't be necessary. To this day, his words fairly reverberate in the chambers of my mind, the echo still audible.

"You were right! The doctors were wrong! It has nothing to do with alcohol!" he'd blurted out.

Of course I was right, but only in a limited sense. I was right about what the condition wasn't. Just as Mary could know without the necessity of faith that her child was virgin born, I, too, had known the condition had nothing to do with alcohol or drugs. But I'd never imagined what it was. In fact, prior to that eventful evening, I'd not known such a condition existed.

Years later, I would still be struggling with the circumstances surrounding the diagnostic phase of the illness. I'd given knowledgeable, duly prepared and licensed physicians – my compensated caretakers – a detailed personal profile, including the fact that as a young man during the notorious 60's, I'd spent the entire decade wearing a short-sleeved white shirt and a clip-on tie, commuting to work in downtown Memphis. I later became aware the available medical evidence pointed directly to the unexpected, but not inconceivable medical condition that was slowly but surely sapping my will to live, incrementally draining my life away.

So what had happened?

It seems diagnosis of the uncommon condition required not so much elaborate testing and methodical elimination of other possible candidates as it did an element of suspicion. In other words, if you weren't looking for it, you weren't going to find it. And the default agent of cause – alcohol and/or drug abuse – was one the medical professionals were readily willing to settle upon, summarily dismissing my protestations. Once receptive to the possibility of the condition, the diagnosis was relatively straightforward. In an instant, with nothing changed except everyone's frame of mind, all the pieces of the medical jigsaw puzzle fit neatly into place.

I'd spent months in physical, mental and emotional misery. I'd been trapped in limbo costing me grief, inconvenience, and many thousands of dollars, only to have my hireling caretakers arrive at an answer that had been right under their noses all along. It was an answer whose cost of discovery in time and money was a mere pittance compared to what had already been expended in futility – and all this because no one had suspected the condition.

My first twelve medical experts, including two specialists at a premier, nationally-known clinic, simply dismissed Anna's and my testimony, one actually noting that wives were often part of the conspiracy of denial. As stacked dominoes falling in a row, each had reviewed the evidence, conducted their own redundant battery of tests, and elected to affirm the conclusions of their colleagues.

Made acutely aware of my frustration, the twelfth and next-to-last doctor embracing the default diagnosis was obviously embarrassed and hesitating in asking my understanding of his and his colleagues' consentient position. He even meekly explained to me how I fit the profile of the classic closet alcohol and drug abuser – right down to my age, profession, and the full beard that I wore.

On that damp September morning, sitting in the pale gold recliner beside my window on the world, none of that mattered anymore. At last, Anna and I knew the name of the beast.

CHAPTER 5

A BEAUTY STATUE COLD

Proud and godly kings . . . built her, long ago,
With . . . towers and tombs and statues all arow . . . .

. . . . Beauty she was statue cold --
there's blood upon her gown. . . .
James Elroy Flecker (1884-1915) *The Dying Patriot*

Everyone has heard the account. What else is there to know? The story of the Tower of Babel is a quaint little homily buttressing the normative version of the origin of the world's many different peoples and languages. For decades, that explanation, baggage dutifully carried with me from the formative years, provided a convenient niche for the incident reported in the eleventh chapter of the book of Genesis. But the theory altered that staid perspective.

The theory holds there's an unfathomed substratum to this nondescript story. Now I saw much more in the curious account of the Tower of Babel. In the mildly entertaining historical account, I now saw vibrant, apocalyptic prophecy. I saw in the story the prophecy of a well-intentioned people's most natural predisposition to settle into a stultifying self-satisfaction. And I saw a drama currently being played out, in spades, in the modern Christian environs I'd inherited at birth.

The story begins following the great Noachian Flood, when the families of the sons of Noah had repopulated the earth.

Now the whole earth used the same language and the same words. And it came about as they journeyed east, that they found a plain in the land of Shinar and settled there.
Genesis 11:1-2 (NASB)

It's understandable that skeptics should discount the story of the Tower of Babel. Its plausibility is immediately tainted by the improbable ecclesial stipulation that at some time in the ancient past, all the people of the earth used the same language and the same words. Once again my credentials had failed me, for the theory holds the quizzical story of the Tower of Babel has nothing to do with spoken languages.

* * *

The morning's shower had been warm on my face and head, sending a shiver through my body. With water streaming over my face, masking any sound emanating from my throat, I felt the rare freedom to relax my defenses. There were times when I did just that. I felt in control most of the time, marginally confident I could face the devastating clinical outlook and premature death bravely and stoically, but those resolute intervals came and went in an inconstant oscillation, locked in a macabre waltz with most abject despair.

I used a wet towel to wipe the moisture off the bathroom mirror. It did a poor job, but sufficient enough to gaze into the mirror and take a long look at the stooped, haggard image staring back at me. I stood there that morning, gaping at the reflection of a very old, very tired middle-aged man, stunned by the weariness in his face.

* * *

The Hebrew word rendered "language" four times in the story of the Tower of Babel is translated as such on just two other occasions in the NASB. These occurrences, however, provide clues to the nature of this universal "language" supposedly common throughout the whole earth at the time of the story. The first of the two, a passage from the book of Isaiah, combines the occurrence of this Hebrew word with the name "Canaan." The translation there is "the language of Canaan."

> **In that day five cities in the land of Egypt will be speaking the language of Canaan and swearing allegiance to the LORD of hosts. . . .** Isaiah 19:18 (NASB)

The symbolism here is absolutely radiant. The infamous five cities of the plain included the familiar Sodom and Gomorrah and are mirrored by the similarly infamous Philistine pentapolis. "Egypt" is almost certainly an archetype of the apostasy identified by Paul as the "falling away," but what was this "language of Canaan" and why was it characterized by the improbable swearing of allegiance to the Hebrew God, the "Lord of hosts"? The theory holds this was prophecy of a pagan form of obeisance, the object of which was not an idol in the ancient sense, but the God of the Hebrews, the "Lord of hosts." And just who – or what – was "Canaan?"

Canaanites were the inhabitants of the Old Testament Promised Land before the conquests by Joshua and the armies of the children of Israel. They were a polytheistic people whose land was dotted with walled cities. They worshiped their many gods with elaborate ritual. Various kinds of authoritative personnel officiated at their ritualistic religious services. These personnel included singers who sang using prescribed forms or psalms and priest-scribes who were responsible for preserving important traditions. Their religion was characterized by many different places of worship, which ranged from humble outdoor settings to massive stone temples reaching to the sky. And with this awareness, the amorphous "language of Canaan" begins to assume recognizable shape and form.

* * *

Barfield Landing, Mississippi County, Arkansas
Summer, 1949

There were banks and sandbars along every other bend in the Mississippi River, which was just behind the levee a city block east of the cracker box on North Pearl Street. With the silvery leaves of the cottonwood groves flashing in the sun and rattling in the water-cooled breeze, Dwayne and I put our names and addresses on slips of paper, sealed them in jars or bottles we had brought from home, and set them adrift in the mighty river. None of them ever came back to us, but I knew there were others like us out there. On one of those frequent adventures to the riverbank, Dwayne's older brother, Charlie Gee, had found a partially buried bottle on a sandbar that contained a slip of paper with a name, address, and launch date. From three years earlier and one-hundred miles upriver in Kentucky, Charlie Gee and the stranger made contact. The stranger's missive had come back to him over time and distance. He had been heard. That was all any of us wanted.

Dwayne and I engaged in some risky adventure, but we knew better than to wade out into the river. Too many people, not all of them kids, where killed attempting recreation in the river. Gently swirling, eighteen-inch-deep muddy water could drop-off to eight feet or more in a single step. The bottom was constantly morphing, and the current wouldn't let even the strongest swimmer come back. The only way to survive was to go with the current and try to paddle to a remote sandbar a mile or more downstream. A few fishermen occasionally ventured onto the river in fishing boats, but that presented an entirely different array of danger.

*

Chester Eakins didn't often include me on fishing junkets with him and his friends. What possessed him to do so on that warm, eventful day in my early youth, I can't say. It's possible it was something Helen Eakins had said. Helen Eakins rarely fished and never enjoyed that, but she was incessantly urging Chester to include me in ostensibly wholesome father-and-son activities such as fishing. If it was at her instigation, she couldn't possibly have known where – and how – we would be fishing. Chester Eakins; my uncle, Arthur Eakins, Chester's closest brother; and an insistent Doc Davis, a friend and business associate of my father, set out with me in tow early that summer morning to go blocking on the mile-wide Mississippi River.

* * *

Nor aught availed him now
To have built in heav'n high tow'rs nor did he scape
By all his engines, but was headlong sent
With his industrious crew to build in hell.
John Milton (1608-1674) *Paradise Lost*, bk.i.l.748

Speaking of Joseph's sojourn in Egypt, an obvious reference to the Egyptian captivity of the children of Israel, the psalmist records,

I heard a language that I did not know. . . . Psalms 81:5 (NASB)

The Hebrew word rendered "language" here is the same word used in the account of the Tower of Babel and identified with "Canaan" in the passage from the book of Isaiah. Again, it's associated with Egypt. The theory suggests the path of understanding runs through the farewell remarks of Joshua made to the children of Israel . . . .

"Now therefore fear the Lord, and serve him in sincerity and in truth; and put away the gods which your fathers served on the other side of the flood, and in Egypt; and serve ye the Lord.

"And if it seem evil to you to serve the Lord, choose you this day whom ye will serve; whether the gods which your fathers served that were on the other side of the flood, or the gods of the Amorites, in whose land ye dwell; but as for me and my house, we will serve the Lord." Joshua 24:14-15 (KJV)

The word translated "flood" here is correctly rendered "River," i.e., the Euphrates, in the NASB. The theory holds this is a reference to Shinar and the plain where the pilgrims of the Tower of Babel story initially settled. At the time of the story, Shinar was inhabited by Sumerians. The Sumerians had in place a system of gods, each with a main temple in a particular city. These were the people among whom the pilgrims of the Tower of Babel story wished to have a name.

That Joshua was referring to the past practice of honoring Egyptian gods by the Israelites during the Egyptian captivity seems certain. That he also referred to the practices of their common ancestors in the land of Shinar, "on the other side of the flood" (i.e., the Euphrates River), seems likewise certain. There was, therefore, a common, chronological thread running from religious practices in Shinar at the time of the construction of the Tower of Babel, through Egypt and the Captivity to the land of the Canaanites at the time of the conquests by Joshua. The theory submits this thread was the mysterious "language" spoken by the whole world, i.e., Babylon (Shinar) and Egypt, connected by the land bridge of Canaan (Palestine).

The theory concludes this Hebrew word (and all occurrences of the translated word "language" in the eleventh chapter of the book of Genesis) is not associated with linguistics, but is rather associated with a religious vein characterized by a stylized homage offered at many different locations in varied temples of wood and stone.

While the "language" used throughout the whole world following the Noachian Flood, up to and including the time of the incident on the plain of Shinar, may or may not have been a spoken dialect, it was most certainly a state of mind. It characterized a mindset given to a stylized, temple-based, ceremonial homage that would in some antitypal "Egypt" swear allegiance, not to an idol, but to the Israelite God, the Lord of hosts. The theory holds the pilgrims who settled on the plain of Shinar to begin construction on the Tower of Babel were initiates of a serially iterative pattern that would be continuous throughout the history of man, up to and including this very day.

* * *

Arthur was the fifth son of Ida and John Eakins. Chester was the seventh and last. There were no girls. Of the brothers, these two were most similar in temperament and stature. Both stood just under six-feet tall, both weighed about 240 pounds.

Doc Davis was considerably less than six-feet tall and wiry. Doc was pretty old, or so I thought at the time – in his seventies. In his younger days, he'd been a vaudevillian and a snake-oil salesman, from whence came his penchant for showmanship and his alias, "Doc." He was remarkably energetic for his age and could still jump a picket fence from a flatfooted stance. Doc wouldn't have weighed more than 150 pounds.

Then, of course, there was me, by that time about average in height and weight for my age. With a four-man crew weighing over seven-hundred pounds, there was little doubt our small craft was overcrowded and overweight, but if anybody was concerned, I wasn't aware of it.

* * *

'Le continuel ouvrage de votre vie,
c'est batir la mort.'
The ceaseless labour of your life
is to build the house of death.
Montaigne (1522-1592) *Essais*, I.xx

The ancient Hebrew account of the Tower of Babel continues:

And they said to one another,

"Come, let us make bricks and burn them thoroughly."

And they used brick for stone, and they used tar for mortar.
And they said,

> **"Come, let us build for ourselves a city and a tower whose top will reach into heaven, and let us make for ourselves a name; lest we be scattered abroad over the face of the whole earth."**

And the Lord came down to see the city and the tower which the sons of men had built. Genesis 11:3-5 (NASB)

There's little doubt the tower was intended to be a permanent installation, but the grandiose proportions ascribed to it are without justification. The word rendered "heaven" in the account is often rendered "sky," and the fired brick and bituminous mortar mentioned as components of the tower were the materials of all moderate Babylonian building projects. The fact that the great Ziggurat at Ur was constructed of those materials doesn't imply that this tower was similarly enormous. The same Hebrew word for "tower" is used in the book of Nehemiah and rendered there as "podium."

The word translated "city" in the account is similarly rendered on numerous occasions in the ancient Hebrew record – but there's a remarkable exception. In the tenth chapter of the book of Second Kings, Jehu's guard and royal officers are commanded to enter the house of Baal in a planned massacre of the followers of Baal.

Then . . . Jehu said to the guard and the royal officers,

> **"Go in, kill them; let none come out."**

And they killed them with the edge of the sword; and the guard and the royal officers threw them out and went to the inner room of the house of Baal. 2 Kings 10:25 (NASB)

The single Hebrew word that's rendered "inner room" is the same word translated "city" in the eleventh chapter of the book of Genesis. Although translated as "inner room" only this once by the NASB, its use here indicates this word was also used to refer to the inner sanctuary of an idolatrous temple.

* * *

Blocking is also known as "jugging," which is more descriptive of the particular type of fishing we would be doing that day. The goal was accomplished by placing a series of floats (jugs) into the water, each of which was affixed with a single weighted, baited hook-and-line. The buoyancy of the float provided all the tension for hooking the beast, playing out line, and the eventual wearing down of the brute. After setting out the floats, you basically just hauled in the fish. It sounds benign enough, but blocking on the Mississippi River at this latitude was dangerous. It required experience with the river, skill with the boat and the mechanics of deployment and recovery of the floats, and occasionally a measure of luck. It didn't happen often, perhaps every generation or so, but locals had been killed while blocking on the Mississippi River.

Chester had ordered about forty closed cylinders which would provide the platform for the day's fishing. The floats were new and painted a bright yellow. Each cylinder was composed of several sealed, empty tin cans welded together end-to-end, thus making a single slender cylinder about twenty-four-inches long with a diameter that of the base of the selected type of can, which appeared to me to be the size of one-quart motor oil cans. On one end of the cylinder, a metal loop was soldered in place. This was where the line was attached. A strong fishing line a few feet in length ran from this loop to a sizeable treble hook.

For the uninitiated, a treble hook is a wicked-looking three-pronged device roughly similar to three fishing hooks stuck together, back to back, with the barbs fanned out equidistant from each other. The sufficiently weighted hook-and-line was then wound tightly around the cylinder for compact storage in the bow of the boat. If the boat was swamped either before deployment or after recovery, everyone on board could be drowned in a tangled morass of brightly colored floats.

The weight used for the lines was ordinary lead, but there was nothing ordinary about the bait. Catfish – especially catfish in the muddy Mississippi River – locate their food primarily by their sense of smell, not sight. Thus the bait has to stink. The worse it stinks, the better it attracts catfish. There were various options, none particularly appealing, but that day we would be using melts.

* * *

Here's the conclusion of the story from the eleventh chapter of the book of Genesis:

And the Lord said,

> **"Behold, they are one people, and they all have the same language. And this is what they begin to do, and now nothing which they purpose will be impossible for them. Come, let Us go down and there confuse their language, that they may not understand one another's speech."**

So the Lord scattered them abroad over the face of the whole earth; and they stopped building the city.

Therefore its name was called Babel [Babylon, "confusion"] because there the Lord confused the language of the whole earth; and from there the Lord scattered them abroad over the face of the whole earth. Genesis 11:6-9 (NASB)

How often I had heard it. In fact, I'd heard it only the day before. On a television commercial for a regional ministry, the preacher stood in the pulpit of his magnificent church building with the splendidly bedecked choir seated behind him.

"When God's people of any church are in agreement, there's nothing that will be impossible for them!" he'd proclaimed with great enthusiasm.

To this the congregation nodded their approval and collectively murmured their "Amen." The man was exhorting his sizeable congregation to unity and the magnificent accomplishments that could be expected therefrom. And he was, no doubt unwittingly, quoting almost exactly from the tower story.

"Behold, they are one . . . and they all have the same language. And this is what they begin to do, and now nothing which they purpose will be impossible for them." Genesis 11:6 (NASB)

Neither he nor his eagerly attentive flock noticed it. For the God-fearing, but woefully misdirected pilgrims on the plain of Shinar, the strength they found in the unity brought by their common "language" wasn't the solution they had supposedly hoped for. It was the problem.

There's an example in the Psalms where the use of the same Hebrew expression indicates the psalmist understood the divine use of "dividing of tongues" to diffuse the undesirable effects of banding together in large groups. There the record reads,

> **Confuse, O Lord, divide their tongues, for I have seen violence and strife in the city.** Psalms 55:9 (NASB)

The expressions "violence and strife," "bloodshed" and/or the "shedding of innocent blood" are often used in the ancient record as metaphors for the neglect of the poor and disadvantaged of God's people and the community-at-large. The implications of the "city" have already been mentioned. (Again, it's the same Hebrew word.) According to the wisdom of the psalmist, the division of tongues and the subsequent scattering – the divine response to the building of the "city" with its tower in the land of Shinar – was the antidote for "violence and strife" in the "city."

* * *

Melts is the name given to stinking, rotten chicken entrails. This bait was free and obtainable by the bucketful from my Uncle Arthur's slaughterhouse and meat packing plant in Portageville. Its success in luring the great river catfish was proven. Perhaps because I lacked usefulness in either the handling of the boat or in the deployment and recovery of the floats, my job on this fishing trip was attaching the stinking, rotten chicken entrails onto those vicious treble hooks.

Even at that time, blocking on the Mississippi River was no longer what it had been in the past. There were fewer large catfish taken than in previous generations, and fuel and other chemical spills in the river had tainted the color and taste of the great river catfish, at least according to some. Decades earlier, a young Elijah Roy had taken individual catfish of around a hundred pounds using this method. A photograph of my father and the eldest of his brothers, taken just a few years earlier, displayed an 80-pounder strung on a pole carried on the shoulders of the two men. We'd be lucky to catch a 10- or 20-pounder this day, but the possibility of a larger catch wasn't totally non-existent.

* * *

Shepherd, I take thy word,
And trust thy honest offer'd courtesy,
Which oft is sooner found in lowly sheds

With smoky rafters, than in tap'stry halls
And courts of princes.
John Milton (1608-1674) *Comus* (1634), l.321

I'd always associated unity with strength and division (or scattering) with weakness, just as the clergy does today when proudly pointing to the congregation's new construction, and that seems to have been the point exactly. The divine response to the settlement on the broad plain of Shinar and the commencement of construction on the "city" with its "tower" was not to encourage, but to *negate* the always misdirected strength born of such unity. The divine will, on the other hand, was implemented by forcing upon the pilgrims a deliberate setting of weakness by scattering them – without their desired fixed, tangible badge of identity – among the peoples of the earth.

The divine response to Paul's request for relief from an unknown malady, his mysterious "thorn in the flesh," becomes clearer with the understanding of the divine use of weakness to negate misdirected strength.

> . . ."**My grace is sufficient . . . for My strength is made perfect** [i.e., complete] **in weakness."** 2 Corinthians 12:9a (KJV)

The pilgrims divinely divided in the land of Shinar were scattered abroad over the face of the earth, just as they had at first feared they would be, dispersed without their distinctive, fixed badge of identity, the "city" (sanctuary) and "tower" (steeple) reaching into the sky which they had inherently desired. In a later cycle, much the same thing happened again following the death of the first Christian martyr, Stephen.[16] The new converts to "the way" were scattered abroad, neither possessing nor positioned to possess a fixed, tangible symbol of identity and focal point for their common faith, a "city" and "tower."

* * *

Upon reaching the desired location in the relatively narrow, deep-water channel, the weighted, baited floats were rapidly deployed over the side of the boat. The instantly plunging weights swiftly uncoiled the lines, the bright yellow cylinders spinning in the water as the line played out, each throwing up a fine spray referred to as a "rooster's tail." Once deployed, the floats were allowed to drift, preferably in a tight formation, with the current of the river.

Using the outboard motor, Chester Eakins raced us downstream, the bow spray and water-cooled air delightful upon my face. He then turned us back into the swift current, holding the boat steady – geostationary, so to speak – as the current carried the flotilla toward our position.

The floats were designed so that when a catfish took the bait, the yellow cylinder would pop straight up in the water, often with an audible crack. They would then bob and weave frantically, occasionally even disappearing briefly beneath the surface. When having especially good luck, several such floats might be bobbing and weaving at the same time. I'd experienced such luck while blocking with my Uncle Arthur in the difficult to reach, but safer pools of the Big Lake swamp, where we'd caught many large grinnel. It was quite a rush.

The most dramatic moment would occur when the boat slowly approached a rocking, bobbing float. The arrested beast, no doubt alert to the close proximity of the boat, would sound, taking the line and the entire float out of sight into the muddy water beneath the boat, just beyond the reach of my outstretched hand. It was enough to make a kid want to go to sea, whaling.

* * *

> **Their land has . . . been filled with idols; they worship the work of their hands, that which their fingers have made. So the common man has been humbled, and the man of importance has been abased. . . .** Isaiah 2:8-9a (NASB)

The theory holds the story of the Tower of Babel to be the prophetic tracing of a pattern, a paradigm illustrative of the uninterrupted collision between man and God, between the carnal and the spiritual. This collision centers on the essence of true homage, described by Jesus in addressing the woman at the well:

> **". . . the hour cometh, and now is, when the true worshippers shall worship the Father in spirit and in truth: for the Father seeketh such to worship him."** John 4:23 (KJV)

The theory suggests the Shinar pilgrimage, as so many others that have followed, began with an aggregate of well-intentioned individuals engaged in a legitimate search for a better country, seeking the true and living God just as that same true and living God called them, but since at least the fourth-century, these Christian pilgrimages have ended in the same way – with settlement and construction upon reaching a "smooth, broad plain." In such an environment, man's inherent drift toward the temple-based homage characteristic of the ancient Sumerians, Babylonians, Egyptians, Canaanites, Greeks, and Romans has its maximal opportunity. Arrival is immediately followed by initiation of plans for a distinctive, fixed badge of identity and focal point for the shared faith. The seekers, thus diverted from their presumed objective of material evangelistic and benevolent service, prematurely end (either completely or substantially) their sojourn by physically constructing their "city" and "tower" which reaches into the sky. This real estate, this monument of wood and stone, concrete and steel becomes the *de facto* center of their faith, denials notwithstanding.

The assertion can be tested with a hypothetical: destroy any given church building by fire or tornado and deny the right to rebuild or replace it. The theory predicts the congregation will dissolve and individuals will relocate. This will occur because the structure is, in fact, that which holds the modern congregation together, not its shared faith.

Vain the ambition of kings
Who seek by trophies and dead things,
To leave a living name behind,
And weave but nets to catch the wind.
John Webster (1580?-1625?) *The Devil's Law-Case*, V. iv

The theory suggests the modern "city" and "tower" thus constructed are fulfillment of prophecy designating a distinctive architecture, one common to pagan cultures from time immemorial, the beloved sanctuary and spire common to Canaanite temples, Roman basilicas, Gothic cathedrals, and now modern Christian edifices.

The Genesis story of the Tower of Babel was prophecy Jesus understood well when dividing the multitude into groups of fifty to one-hundred at the feeding of the five-thousand. The theory suggests that directive was neither arbitrary nor convenient, but exemplary. Groups of fifty to one-hundred are small enough to provide for effective leadership and personal service with neither the necessity nor the collective means to invest limited human and material resources into gluttonous real estate and staffing requirements.

***

The hazards which characterized blocking on the Mississippi River at this latitude were the result of the swift, unpredictable current and floating debris in the river, often barely visible even upon close approach. And then, of course, there were the barges.

The great river tows were a sight to behold. A hundred feet wide and a thousand feet long, the tows were the unchallenged lords of the river. They were large and powerful, transporting up to twenty-thousand tons of cargo, as much as a fully loaded freight train four miles long, and when plying up the narrow, deep-water channel behind perhaps twenty-four units tightly lashed together into a single three-acre module, a locomotive probably had as much maneuverability.

When such a rig came into view around the bend, perhaps a mile south of our position, Chester Eakins had two choices. The safest was to promptly leave the channel and get well out of the way, allowing the tow to overrun and scatter the floats, inevitably resulting in the loss of a sizeable portion of the flotilla and considerable time. The other choice was to hurriedly recover the floats and store them on board, redeploying the full complement after the tow had passed. When electing the latter choice, any capsizing due to collision with submerged debris or heavy-handed fumbling of an attempt to restart a stalled motor could plunge everyone from fishermen to tow crew into desperate crisis.

Tow captains immediately recognized the potential for disaster upon catching first sight of a fishing rig such as ours. The booming air horn would sound long and hard, scoldingly and angrily as the small boat scurried to and fro to recover the flotilla in the few moments before the tow overran the position.

***

What is a church?---Our honest sexton tells,
'Tis a tall building, with a tower and bells.
George Crabbe (1754-1832) *The Borough*, letter ii, *The Church*, l.11

If the Genesis story of the Tower of Babel foreshadowed the rise and solidification of temple-based homage in post-fourth-century Christianity (the "plain of Shinar" being archetype of the Constantinian sanction of 313), what then was the model for its implied antithesis?

The record tells us God sent a message to King David through the prophet Nathan regarding the assembly of the congregation, the body of believers, the "house" for the name of the Lord:

> **". . . I will set up thy seed after thee, which shall proceed out of thy bowels, and I will establish his kingdom. He shall build an house for my name, and I will stablish the throne of his kingdom for ever. I will be his father, and he shall be my son."**
> 2 Samuel 7:12b-14a (KJV)

The direct reference was to David's son and heir, Solomon, but the ancient record prophesied more, a later cycle where the singular, magnificent structure known as Solomon's Temple was archetype of another "house" or dwelling place of the name of God. The writer of the book of Hebrews was obviously referring to Jesus when he made reference to the passage above . . .

> **For unto which of the angels said he . . .**
>
> > **"I will be to him a Father, and he shall be to me a Son?"** Hebrews 1:5 (KJV)

Solomon built a splendid material Temple. The task of the antitypal Messiah in a later cycle was not to build many material temples, but to build a similarly splendid one – a spiritual temple, a spiritual house, the sanctuary and residence of the living God.

> **. . . as he went out of the temple, one of his disciples saith unto him,**
>
> > **"Master, see what manner of stones and what buildings are here!"**
>
> **And Jesus answering said unto him,**
>
> > **"Seest thou these great buildings? there shall not be left one stone upon another, that shall not be thrown down."** Mark 13:1-2 (KJV)

Some say Jesus was prophesying the destruction of Herod's Temple by the Romans, which did, in fact, occur about forty years later. Perhaps he was, but the theory suggests he was prophesying something more, another antitype. The theory holds Jesus was speaking of an era when temple-based homage would be ended, even that of the uniquely singular Temple at Jerusalem. He spoke of an era when God would not be honored in temples of wood and stone or concrete and steel, not in the “high (lofty) places” of the Canaanites, neither in a Solomon's, nor a Zerubbabel's, nor a Herod's Temple, the one standing in magnificence during the days of Jesus. The theory suggests he was describing an era when God would be honored “neither in this mountain nor in Jerusalem,”[17] neither here nor there, but everywhere, at every time and in every place where the believer was present. He was describing a movement, not an institution.

Early Christians understood this well, for there was no directive and no attempt to duplicate the pagan shrines or the Jewish synagogues (also destroyed in the Jewish War of 67-73 C.E.) by those who knew Jesus most intimately. There was, in fact, no “plain of Shinar” until the advent of the Constantinian sanction in the early-fourth-century.

* * *

The tales of local fishermen and their boats being run down by the tows were haunting. The consequences of a mid-current stopping of the great engines powering the barge train or deliberately running the tow aground could be unbelievable. Without the thrust of the powerful engines, the tow would spin out of control, falling away downstream as a stalled airplane falls over its high wing into a graveyard spiral. Upon striking a shallow sand bar, the tow could break up, creating a nightmare for tows further downstream until the runaway barges could be corralled or run aground. Even then, the damage could continue. The vagary of the water level on the river meant it could take weeks, perhaps months, to refloat the beached units and unwind the damage. Even worse, rising water could send beached units silently cartwheeling downstream into the path of northbound tows at any time of day or night. Given these potential consequences, the irritation in the warning blasts coming from the tow had ample justification.

Although not beyond attempting a recovery in the path of the tow, Chester Eakins' choice that day was the safe one, even though it meant losing tens of minutes fishing time and a significant portion of the flotilla. He maneuvered our small boat into a safe, quiet area of the river where we sat idle, watching as the tow ripped through the heart of the flotilla.

*

The wake left by the great river tows, fanning out from the wash of the powerful engines, is spectacular to see when standing on the bluff overlooking the river. I was not aware of it at the time, but it takes that special vantage to appreciate the severity and duration of the wake, for such insight is not available from the surface. I suppose altitude above the surface of the river and the distinct angle of view enhances perception of the amplitude of the trailing wake by means of light and shadow. From the surface of the river, that deadly wake is practically invisible until it is immediately upon you.

After giving the tow a respectably wide berth, Chester Eakins once again maneuvered our open boat back toward the main channel. He was now seeking to recover the remnants of the flotilla as soon as possible, for by this time they were scattered over an area approaching a half-mile square.

The tow was moving upstream, well past our position, the drone of its great engines noticeably decreased in intensity. Just as I felt in my heart the assurance of a crisis wisely averted, the image of that monster wake, totally invisible a heartbeat ago, swelling up from the surface of that great, wide river struck cold terror into my heart. In an instant, right before the bow, only a few feet away and seeming to emanate out of the placid stillness of the surface like the emerging spine of a gigantic sea monster, there arose an enormous swell, the crest seemingly as high as our heads.

We hadn't seen it, hadn't anticipated it this far behind the tow. All of us, the experienced and the neophyte, had believed we were far enough behind the tow for the river to have smoothed. Without the play of light and shadow available with elevation and angle, we hadn't seen that residual wake, still roily, still formidable.

* * *

When you . . . have remained long in the land . . . and make an idol in the form of anything . . . so as to provoke Him . . . you shall surely perish quickly from the land . . . and . . . shall serve gods, the work of man's hands, wood and stone, which neither see nor hear nor eat nor smell. Deuteronomy 4:25-28 (NASB)

By the assimilation of alien, incompatible entities, a deadly strain is introduced into the organism. In this case, it was something that carried with it the seeds of spiritual "death," i.e., expulsion or exclusion, from the kingdom of God, the New Testament promised land in real time.

Within a hundred years following Constantine's conversion and his legitimization of Christianity, excessive wealth, power and luxury had eroded the integrity of the Church. Clerics with a thirst for power and control, fought for candidates to the offices of the Church on the basis of family prominence, partisanship, or wealth. Others supported the candidacy of friends, relatives, and flatterers. Character was not a primary attribute. By the Middle Ages, a counterfeit form of Christianity had evolved. Gothic church structures and cathedrals dotted the European and Middle Eastern landscape, conveniently providing a consolidated power base for the feudal organization of Church and state that existed at the time.

The Protestant Reformation and later similar efforts were indeed intended as corrective shifts in position, but along the same linear alignment which preserved the post-Constantinian model of the Church. The theory holds the simple beauty of "the way" is apparent only by a lateral, parallactic shift away from that alignment.

* * *

There were three truly large, periodic waves in rapid succession. Each seemed as though it would swamp our small boat and in an instant, in a split-second, bring the mile-wide surface of the Mississippi River right up to our ears.

With a tremendous upsurge, the first wave lifted us like an express elevator to the penthouse, sucking the breath right out of my lungs. Almost instantly, the bow pitched downward, the drop as swift as that of a gallows' floor, leaving my heart in my throat and a supercooled lump in the pit of my stomach. There was a bone-jarring crash as the bow slammed into the first trough. Instantly, the surface of that great, wide river rose right up to the gunnels as we were heaved upward again, then pitched down into the following trough. We were caught up in a quarter-mile-long roller coaster ride compressed into about fifty feet.

It was over in a few desperate seconds. Nobody had spoken a word during the moment of stunned surprise before the wake hit or during the desperation of the battering that followed. We were dripping wet from the splash and water swirled about our ankles in the bottom of the boat, but the craft wasn't swamped. My heart beat as though it would burst through my soaked shirt. Even now, my pulse quickens when I recount the moment. Even now, though I later became an accomplished swimmer and a Red Cross lifeguard, one of my greatest fears remains that of a tide of rapidly rising water.

We actually caught a few small catfish that day, but I never again went fishing on the river. To my knowledge, neither did Chester Eakins. And neither of us ever rehashed the events of that day. I'm certain Helen Eakins never knew.

* * *

> **"Do you become a king because you are competing in cedar? Did not your father eat and drink and do justice and righteousness? Then it was well with him. He pled the cause of the afflicted and needy; then it was well. Is not that what it means to know Me?"** Jeremiah 22:15-16 (NASB)

The gods of mankind are always fashioned in the image of whatever is precious to their makers. Over the two-thousand years since the advent of Messiah, the idols of ancient man have not been so much discarded as transmuted, as the notions of those who fashion them have evolved. Thus, the images and values of the temples themselves have in modern times replaced the images of the local deities known then as the Baals. Confronted with the distraction of these extravagancies of Christian piety, the homage of service Jesus of Nazareth both taught and demonstrated is submerged in a tide of vanity and pride, shrouded with the cloak of an inanimate presence, a beauty statue cold.

The theory holds these church buildings, these monuments of wood and stone, concrete and steel that neither see, nor hear, nor eat, nor smell, expressly or implicitly built to the glory of a living God, are, in fact, great engines of revenue and consumption, just as their counterparts in the world of commercial real estate. They're designed to generate and, of necessity, consume resources of time and money – in this case, the Christian tithe – intended to relieve human misery and to deliver by word and deed, individually and collectively, Jesus' message of

Christian character epitomized by a reverence of God and good deeds toward man. But wherever they are found, these parcels of real estate and their accouterments become their respective pilgrims' badge of identity, consuming in debt service, maintenance, and staffing requirements a substantial majority of the tithe thus gathered, until the god so honored becomes a crass materialism, inimitably captured in the adornments of the Church.

*

With aching hands and bleeding feet
We dig and heap, lay stone on stone;
We bear the burden and the heat
Of the long day, and wish 'twere done.
Not till the hours of light return,
All we have built do we discern.
Matthew Arnold (1822-1888) *Mortality*, st.2.

Whether wisdom and understanding or folly, I leave that to others to judge. Projected to a vantage point above the massive flow, I saw that which hadn't been apparent from the surface. In such a manner, wisdom and understanding – or folly, such as it may be – became mine, defining who and what I would be for the remainder of my life.

* * *

As though by catapult, I was exploded from the time capsule wherein I'd retreated and once again forcefully snatched from my reverie. My gaze flashed to the interior of the room, and the kaleidoscope of color and harmony of sound that had held my fascination captive dissolved instantaneously. Chiming with the somber periodicity that proved to be the harbinger of the Ghost of Christmas Yet To Come, the wall clock in the foyer struck ten times, then receded into silence. As though an angel thundered, I heard and felt the marker signaling celerity, the token that summoned me forth from all that was past and forced upon me once again all that was present and real. Anna – and Rebekah and Jared – would be home soon. Soon it would be time to go. Soon I would have to leave the pale gold recliner and my window on the world to go where I didn't want to go and submit to a destiny I had hoped, by all means, to avoid.

CHAPTER 6

THE NEWER RITE

Tantum ergo sacramentum
Veneremur cernui;
Et antiquum documentum
Novo cedat ritui.
Therefore we, before him bending,
This great Sacrament revere;
Types and shadows have their ending,
For the newer rite is here.
St. Thomas Aquinas c.1225-1274, *English Hymnal*, 326

Among the varied, hallowed rites of Christendom, there is none more reverential, none more portentous than the Lord's Supper, also known as Communion or the Eucharist. The Lord's Supper is of particular import here because the New Testament reveals its abuse carried with it immediate, recognizable consequences.

Silent and amazed even when a little boy,
I remember I heard the preacher every Sunday
put God in his statements,
As contending against some being or influence.
Walt Whitman (1819-1892) *A Child's Amaze*

I'd been there in church every Sunday morning, sitting beside Helen Eakins when the shiny silver trays bearing first the unleavened bread and then the cup were first blessed and then passed from hand to hand and from pew to pew throughout the congregation. I'd watched in reverential awe as she carefully received the first tray, pinched a pea-sized crumb from the wafer of unleavened bread and placed it on her tongue. And when the second tray was passed, again I stared, transfixed as her hand gently lifted the tiny, clear-glass cup with the flanged rim, the carefully measured burgundy contents of any given cup capable of little more than moistening the lips.

Visitors were explicitly welcome to attend all regular services of the church. They could join in the singing of hymns and bowing of heads in communal prayer, dutifully listen to and consider the words of the preacher, and even place a contribution in the collection plate, if they so desired. But none other than those who had received the baptism of the church were welcome to partake of the Lord's Supper. That exclusivity no doubt added to the mystique.

***

Blytheville, Mississippi County, Arkansas
Summer, 1949

Riding the mercurial fortunes of a super salesman and dealmaker proved a manic-depressive experience. In the summer of '49, Chester Eakins was on a roll. On a clear June day, the family piled into Chester's new Cadillac and traveled north on U.S. 61 eighteen miles to the county seat. Chester had purchased a large, older home on Blytheville's magnificently canopied West Main Street. The street was lined with stately mature trees of various native species whose mushrooming crowns met over the center of the street, giving the traveler the impression he was moving through a shaded tunnel.

Fourteen-year-old Jean, about to become a high school freshman, threw a fit about the move, but with her trademark resiliency, she hit the ground with her feet running and never missed a step. Immediately upon our arrival on West Main Street, news of the coming of the pretty, popular girl from Osceola spread among the insiders of Blytheville High School's most favored clique. The girls of BHS Class of '53 came by frequently that summer, picking up Jean in a late model convertible. They would go off for the day, two or three of the girls sitting on the retracted convertible top, just as those same girls would do for the many parades that characterized our small town existence in the early '50's.

***

So may the outward shows be least themselves:
The world is still deceived with ornament.
In law, what plea so tainted and corrupt
But, being season'd with a gracious voice,
Obscures the show of evil? In religion,
What damned error, but some sober brow

Will bless it and approve it with a text,
Hiding the grossness with fair ornament?

There is no vice so simple but assumes
Some mark of virtue on his outward parts.
William Shakespeare, *Merchant of Venice*, III.ii.73

All the homage of religion is supremely solemn and venerable in the eyes of a child. I was mesmerized by the communion ritual and remained spellbound by it and other rites of the church for as long as I remained a child. There was, you see, first in me that inherent proclivity, that genetic bias, for the ceremonial deference characteristic of pagan rites in general and the stylized oblations of the antecedent Canaanite inhabitants of the Promised Land in specific. It was a reverence of deity composed more of symbol and rite than of substance and agency. In time, I would become a man, willing and able to put away such deference. But that would be decades later, after twenty-two years struggling as a churchman-in-good-standing and another fifteen years in search of a seemingly elusive God as a silent constituent of the indeterminable unchurched in America. Only after I should have died did I become alive to the distinctions Jesus of Nazareth had so carefully crafted.

* * *

Twelve days earlier, I'd slumped to the dining room floor, having had just enough consciousness to telephone Anna at her office and tell her I was again hemorrhaging internally and needed help. I'd been sitting on the white divan in our living room shortly before noon, reading the morning's newspaper, basking in the brief, periodic respite from the low-grade fever, when I recognized that first faint sensation, that twinge that told me it was happening again. It's strange how there was no mistaking that feeling, that certain, instantaneous knowledge that I was once again in serious trouble. In a moment, in the twinkling of an eye, the gaunt, hooded ferryman was again standing at the door.

I'd spoken to Anna in a tone I thought rational and calm. She was talking excitedly, frantically launching questions regarding the symptoms I was experiencing. At some point, I realized that, although hearing her, my lips weren't responding to her urgent appeal for information. I slowly slipped down the facing of the archway between the kitchen and the dining room, momentarily sitting upright against the post before slowly and softly rolling forward onto the carpeted dining room floor. I'd been conscious all the way down, but without any control over what was happening.

I lay there on one shoulder, my head resting on the floor, listening to Anna's desperate voice coming from the spilled handset lying on the floor beside me, alert to her urgent attempts to secure a further response from me, but unable to answer. My mind heard her, my spirit wanted to speak and reassure her, but nothing came forth. My lips wouldn't form the words my brain was commanding. My body rested there on the floor, my mind hypnotized by the imploring voice coming from the handset.

*

Anna had hung up and the spiral-corded hand piece was emitting a loud, steady dial tone. I was only vaguely aware of it. I was conscious, and I knew where I was. I was on the dining room floor. Mentally, however, I was far away, drifting alone on the gentle swells of an ethereal sea. I was still there on the floor, drifting with the currents, when Anna and her office supervisor, Shelly Mitchell, came through the front door.

* * *

There lives more faith in honest doubt,
Believe me, than in half the creeds.

Alfred, Lord Tennyson (1809-1892) *In Memoriam A.H.H.* (1850), xcvi

Doubt was the courtyard through which I had to pass if I would approach the temple of wisdom. I'd genuinely believed I could fulfill the Christian commitment by adherence to church doctrine. In doing so, I had gained and maintained the favor of everyone around me, but there wasn't a shred of evidence to suggest God had taken notice.

It wasn't enough for me, being spoon-fed that glorious tradition, the victuals of that venerable democracy of the dead. My intelligence hadn't calcified. I actually thought it was up to me to prove it all over again. Good student that I'd always been, I poured over the record and pondered what I read there. Without the awareness of having done anything other than what I'd always been led to believe was the mark of a good Christian, I surprisingly found myself provoking the annoyance and even the suspicion of the church leadership.

*

It seemed to me the approach of the church – and indeed all existing ecclesiologic theory – to describing and predicting the modern Christian experience was effectively to ignore it. Neglecting the obvious effects of unrecognized quantities, they chose to simplistically represent them by convenient platitudes such as "God works in mysterious ways" or summarily dismiss them as a test of Christian character. But sound reasoning made it impossible to confirm a valid theory by reinventing or recycling extant ecclesiastic theories that explain and predict the Christian experience only by reliance upon venerable tradition. In the ancient record, there is no course more treacherous. The ultimate theory, like any good theory, will be characterized by the fact that it makes predictions that can be verified by observation and experience.

The power of punishment is to silence, not to confute.
Samuel Johnson (1709-1784) *Sermons*, No. xxiii

The growing doubt within me was not doubt of God, Jesus or of the Holy Spirit. It was doubt of the late-twentieth-century institution championed as the Church. It was the initial outcropping of a desperate need for understanding that was being routinely denied me by the clergy and the senior laity, who were conditioned by long practice to fit rifts in the doctrine of the church with the hush of an effective silencer conveniently labeled "faith."

I was tacitly undergoing transformation, as if from proton to neutron, evolving beyond the nuclear core of my matriarchal sect. In time, I emerged a constituent of opposite charge, held in unstable orbit only by the invisible force that was my vested late-twentieth-century Christian heritage.

Had I been willing to remain part of the nuclear triad that comprised the church as aggressively positive, passively neutral, or even doubtfully negative (held, of course, in proper orbit by the attraction of the nuclear core), the church would've allowed me to stay. In the end, it wasn't necessary. I couldn't stay.

I made the break amid the tyranny of the '70s labeled self-actualization, deliberately choosing the disparaged existence of Christian expatriate.

* * *

I believe he would perform the operation for the stone -- build St. Peter's -- or assume (with or without ten minutes' notice) the command of the Channel Fleet; and no one would discover by his manner that the patient had died -- the church tumbled down -- and the Channel Fleet been knocked to atoms.

Revd. Sydney Smith (1771-1845), spoken of Lord John Russell, *Works* (1859), vol. ii, Second letter to Arch-deacon Singleton, 1838, p.275

Chester Eakins was a natural, the quintessential framer of the deal. He was never taught it. It was ingrained in the fabric of the man.

A "deal" was a proposed or completed transaction, most often involving farm real estate, but he extended the use of the term to every facet of life. He was always looking to make the deal. The deal was undiluted excitement to him, his only god, his only reason for existence.

He was born in 1915 and came into manhood during the Great Depression, a son of the American heartland. Typical of a great many of his generation, his most gratifying achievement was the repayment of his legitimate debts. He took fierce pride in paying what he owed, as though it was the measure of his worth as a man, and perhaps it was. If he couldn't pay on time, he was there negotiating an extension, and if that failed, then a refinancing by a third party. Honesty and hard work were his only Bible and the "deal" his only calling.

He was an early riser, consistent with the profile of the successful type. In the pre-dawn darkness of a frosty winter morning, he could be found in the old Cotton Boll Cafe on East Main Street in Blytheville. He'd sit there, drinking black coffee and chewing on the stub of his Roi Tan cigar while tapping out a restless, repetitive rhythm with the toes and heels of his quarter-length boots. And all the while, he'd be looking over the nearly empty cafe and impatiently muttering something about nobody wanting to work anymore.

When a major deal fell through after a day of intense negotiation at the old King Cotton Hotel in Memphis, I once saw him offer his wristwatch in exchange for his counterpart's wristwatch, saying with a cocked head, a sheepish grin, and a certain Jimmie Durante pizzazz, "Well, I gotta cheat ya outta somethin'!"

I had to become a seasoned adult to understand how he did it, how he managed to perpetuate the myth that surrounded him, the myth of an infallible Midas touch. He didn't win 'em all, but by the simple act of ignoring his failures and accentuating his successes, he had everyone believing that he did.

* * *

What was the origin of the ritualistic observance central to the late-twentieth-century Christian homage of the church? What was the "Lord's Supper" ordained by Jesus in the upper room and addressed by Paul in his first-century letter to the neophyte Christian congregation in the Greek city of Corinth? Why was it instituted in the first place? When, and why, did its observance become ritualistic rather than substantive? Most sobering, what constituted its abuse, precipitating the immediate, undesirable consequences which befell the Corinthian congregation?

The trouble with people is not that they don't know, but that they know so much that ain't so.
Josh Billings (Henry Wheeler Shaw) (1818-1885)
Josh Billings' Encyclopedia of Wit and Wisdom (1874)

The term, Lord's Supper, is used only once in the New Testament. In the rebuke of the Corinthian assembly for its abuse of the feast, Paul scolded them for a selfishness that had so altered the character of the feast that it no longer qualified as the same observance.

When ye come together therefore into one place, this is not to eat the Lord's supper. 1 Corinthians 11:20 (KJV)

By the time of the early English translations, the sacramentalism characteristic of the matriarchal Church had dominated the Christian landscape for centuries. The fact is the Greek word translated "supper" in this verse is rendered "banquet" or "dinner" when referring to anything other than this specific Corinthian observance. It is the same Greek word rendered "banquet" in the sixth chapter of the book of Mark, where it refers to the infamous bacchanalian feast where the daughter of Herodias danced before Herod Antipas.[18]

The archetype of the celebration is found in the ancient Hebrew record. The Passover celebration of the Israelites was instituted the night of the tenth decisive plague that God brought upon Pharaoh and the Egyptians, the midnight visitation of the death angel and the heartrending death of the firstborn. On that night, the Destroyer is said to have slain the first born of every household, both of man and beast, where the lintel and doorposts were not marked by the blood of the Passover lamb. Those houses protected by the blood of the Passover lamb, the Destroyer did "pass over." God had issued a warning through Moses and Aaron, describing what the Israelites must do to avoid the plague being brought upon their Egyptian overlords. The sacrifice of the Passover lamb and the shared feast associated with it provided the means for the Israelites to insulate themselves from this tenth and decisive plague.

Again the ancient Hebrew record offers up prophecy disguised as history, for in another cycle well over a thousand years later, the sacrificial Passover lamb became irrevocably linked with Jesus, the Messiah, the Lamb of God, the cornerstone of Christianity.

The Passover feast was more than sacramental or ceremonial. It was a full-blown banquet, and it was Jesus' upper room celebration of this banquet with the Twelve the evening before the crucifixion that was being commemorated at Corinth.

* * *

There's a certain Slant of light,
Winter Afternoons --
That compresses like the Heft
Of Cathedral Tunes --
Heavenly Hurt, it gives us --
We can find no scar,
But internal difference,
Where the Meanings, are.

Emily Dickinson (1830-1886) *There's a certain Slant of light*

The condition that was slowly, relentlessly draining from me the spark of life demanded inordinate quantities of idle time in which to cease the blind groping for elusive solutions to seemingly insoluble mysteries and ponder all that had so rapidly rushed by me. At times at strange peace within myself and with the world around me, I consumed quiet mornings and hushed afternoons sitting in the silence of that living room. Overwhelmed by the periodic low-grade fever that visited me in those oddly dependable twelve-hour cycles, I examined patterns made by the sun shining through the trees and watched shadows creep across the carpet.

* * *

In the eighth-century B.C.E., Hezekiah became the thirteenth king of Judah and reigned twenty-nine years in Jerusalem. Many good and worthwhile amends came about because of his reformations, but the one of most interest here is the reinstitution of the long-neglected Passover feast.

Hezekiah brought in the priests and Levites, gathering them on the square east of Solomon's Temple, and made a remarkable comment. He told them the priests' and Levites' ancestors had brought wrath (bad things) upon Judah. He commanded the priests and Levites to begin consecrating themselves to cleanse the Temple in order that the Lord's anger might turn away, that they might once again gain the protective shelter of God.

A similar situation occurred years later under the reign of Josiah. Josiah was the sixteenth king of Judah and reigned three decades in the seventh-century B.C.E. In the eighteenth year of his reign, a copy of the book of the Law was discovered during repair of the Temple. When the king heard the words of the Law, he expressed extreme distress. These were his words:

> **"Go, inquire of the LORD for me and for them that are left in Israel and in Judah concerning the words of the book that is found: for great is the wrath of the LORD that is poured out upon us, because our fathers have not kept the word of the LORD, to do after all that is written in this book."**
>
> 2 Chronicles 34:21 (KJV)

The circumstances here repeat themselves almost identically. Clerical ancestors had failed their followers, wrath (bad things) was upon the people, and a wise leader formulated a corrective action.

The king gathered all the elders of Judah and Jerusalem and read in their hearing all the words of the book that was found in the house of the Lord. Then the king stood in his place and promised before the Lord to walk after him, his testimonies, and his statutes with all his heart and with all his soul. All present stood with him and, according to the ancient record, Josiah thereby removed the offense of the children of Israel.

When the Passover banquet was prepared, food was carried to the laity first and only afterwards to the priests and Levites.

> **. . . they [the Levites] roasted the passover with fire according to the ordinance: but the other holy offerings sod they in pots, and in caldrons, and in pans, and divided them speedily among all the people. And afterward they made ready for themselves and for the priests. . . .** 2 Chronicles 35:13-14a (KJV)

But notice what was occurring at the flawed Corinthian observance of the Lord's Supper . . .

> **When ye come together therefore into one place, this is not to eat the Lord's supper. For in eating every one taketh before other his own supper . . . What?** 1 Corinthians 11:20-22a (KJV)

It was the ordained Passover pattern of unselfish sharing which the Corinthian congregation was violating, and this to their immediate detriment. The privileged of the Corinthian congregation had, by definition, a well from which to draw their daily necessity, but the unfortunate among the congregation did not. Sporadic, if not complete, neglect was present in the Corinthian observance of the Lord's Supper, without the apparent awareness or concern of the insensitive fortunate set. Those observing the Lord's Supper in the little congregation of the church in Osceola weren't in a position to distinguish need either.

When Jesus said,

> **. . . "this do in remembrance of me". . . .** 1 Corinthians 11:24 (KJV)

hadn't I always assumed he was making reference to a solemn, ceremonial ritual that was being ordained to regularly commemorate his approaching sacrificial death, in effect just another exercise of *eisegesis*, the reading into the text a truth as it has already been perceived?

If the Last Supper on the night in which he was betrayed wasn't an observance of the Hebrew Passover celebration, then what was it? A new ceremonial rite divinely destined to become the focal point of a stylized, ceremonial Gentile worship? Somehow I doubt it. A stylized, token observance of the sharing of things substantive was not in the nature and character of Jesus. The new covenant was about substantive sharing, not the rituals and ceremony characteristic of pagan homage.

The theory suggests all ceremonial ritual is the necessary invention of the emergent clergy, designed to keep the flock at a proper distance. Ritual and ceremony form a perimeter defense for custom and conformity, which would too often be broken in upon if not for such camp wire. To deprive the modern model of the Church of its established ceremonial ritual would almost certainly bring the institution into contempt. But the most damaging characteristic of ritual is not that it's useless or wasteful. It's pernicious because it creates self-deception.

As the Lord's Supper has evolved in the post-Constantinian model of the Church, the suppliant, in the privacy of individual devotion, communes with a God who is somewhere out there as opposed to somewhere in the midst in the form of needful communicants. Was not the celebration of the Lord's Supper instead to join those on the Emmaus road[19] who had no hope left and, in breaking the common bread with a fellow traveler, thus encounter the epiphanic Jesus in their midst?

> **And they drew nigh unto the village, whither they went: and he made as though he would have gone further. But they constrained him, saying,**
>
> > **"Abide with us: for it is toward evening, and the day is far spent."**
>
> **And he went in to tarry with them. And it came to pass, as he sat at meat with them, he took bread and blessed it, and brake, and gave to them. And their eyes were opened, and they knew him. . . .** Luke 24:28-31a (KJV)

* * *

By the spring of '52, the periodic perigee of the super salesman had arrived. Financial exigency forced the sale of the manor house at the prestigious West Main Street address. The family relocated to a new development on the northern edge of town, one only recently created from the cotton fields surrounding Blytheville. The small flagstone, ranch-style house was more commodious than the North Pearl Street cracker box in Osceola, but subordinate to the manor house on West Main Street.

* * *

Exactly when did the feast that was the regular observances of the Lord's Supper become a ceremonial rite instead of the legitimate banquet its prototype had been under the tutorial Hebrew sacrificial system and among first-century Christians? It wasn't at the origin, at the institution of the Passover in Egypt. It wasn't among the first assemblies of the Jerusalem congregation, who went from house to house, sharing their bread. It wasn't at the observance in Corinth, and it wasn't at the communal feasts of fraternal friendship mentioned in the book of Jude. All of these were genuine feasts where those who had abundance offered their sacrifice of thanksgiving to a living God by sharing that abundance with those among their number who had little or nothing. But by the early-second-century, there's historical evidence of ritual being substituted for substance, of ceremony being used to impart a pagan sheen to pallid deeds.

If the question of when cannot be answered with certainty, the same cannot be said of how. How did sharing with the less fortunate of the Christian assembly in a demonstration of joy and thanksgiving for the blessings of God become a sterile religious rite void of tangible substance? The theory suggests the rite evolved through the same marriage of pagan and Christian concepts that has effectively nullified the model of the first-century movement known as "the way."

* * *

In our most desperate moments, Chester Eakins could talk the local banker or a wealthy landowner into a signature loan, guaranteed solely by his unsullied reputation as the ultimate deal maker. The first thing we would do is load the car and leave for a brief, but impressive family vacation to Florida or the Gulf Coast. This may not have been responsible, but it was consistent with the maintaining of the Midas myth. When we were at or near our lowest point, all our neighbors and relatives could see was the family leaving for a vacation in the sun. Chester Eakins, always exuding success even if sporadically experiencing it, lived life on the brink of financial ruin.

* * *

> **For this cause, many are weak and sickly among you, and many sleep.** 1 Corinthians 11:30 (KJV)

Paul warned the Corinthian congregation that their loss of focus in the observance of the Lord's Supper had resulted in many of their number being weak and sick. For this reason a number did, apparently prematurely, "sleep," a commonly used metaphor for death. The Corinthian congregation's health and welfare had begun to resemble that of the pagan community surrounding them. It was their sign, for there's something inherently wrong when one can't tell the Christians' allotment from that of the relatively good, the not-so-good, the obviously bad, and the downright evil. The suggestion that this condition is God's will or the result of his unprovoked neglect is unjustified. The name of God is profaned among the disbeliever because of this.

> **. . . I scattered them among the heathen, and they were dispersed through the countries . . . and . . . whither they went, they profaned my holy name, when they said to them,**
>
> > **"These are the people of the LORD, and are gone forth out of his land."** Ezekiel 36:19-20 (KJV)

From the mainstream, temple-based Christian to the disenfranchised, unchurched Christian to the totally alienated agnostic, hope for light is routinely met with unmistakable darkness. As blind men groping in the dark, either growling like bears or moaning like doves, all look for the mercy and justice of God, finding it inconsistently, if at all. In despair, the cry to God, to deaf heaven, is, "Why?"

> **Thou art indeed just, Lord, if I contend**
> **With thee; but, sir, so what I plead is just.**
> **Why do sinners' ways prosper? and why must**
> **Disappointment all I endeavour end?**
> Gerard Manley Hopkins (1844-1889) *Thou Art Indeed Just, Lord*

From the ancient Hebrew record, the prophet had answered long ago, but I hadn't heard.

> **". . . my people are gone into captivity, because they have no knowledge: and their honourable men are famished, and their multitude dried up with thirst. Therefore hell hath enlarged herself, and opened her mouth without measure: and their glory, and their multitude, and their pomp, and he that rejoiceth, shall descend into it."** Isaiah 5:13-14 (KJV)

These conditions have always existed for those in the community-at-large, but since at least the fourth-century, they've characterized the supposed children of light. The theory holds this is because their estrangement from God has persisted since that time.

Despite corrective efforts, every new wind of doctrine, every nascent spawn of the dam becomes as self-perpetuating as the *materfamilias* that antedates it. The vested interests of its devotees assure its continued existence. The foundational, institutional understructure is never thoughtfully reexamined, much less willfully abandoned as when the apostle Paul modified his pre-Damascus-Road notions of the will and designs of God.

The theory holds all such endeavor, however well-intentioned, is fatally flawed from the outset, there being no possibility of laying claim to the New Testament promised land in real time while embracing the post-Constantinian model. In every such effort, there is very quickly too much invested – too much money, too much time, too much ego – in the highly visible, but intrinsically superficial profile.

No great improvements in the lot of mankind are possible, until a great change takes place in the fundamental constitution of their modes of thought.

John Stuart Mill (1806-1873) *Autobiography* (1873), ch.7

Rather than a panacea for the troubles of the world, the theory holds the Church – as it presents in the post-Constantinian model – can offer little other than psychodramatic relief for the desperate inner need which drives people to seek the sheltered enclaves of the living God.

* * *

As a man freezing to death, whose most urgent wish is to curl up in the snow and go to sleep, I grimly struggled with the consequences of such a decision. As a younger man, I'd prayed for a mission. I'd prayed for the financial means to aid – with food, clothing and shelter – a remarkable foreign missionary who was studying in this country and had crossed my path. Within months, I acquired the resources and, over the span of the next two to three years, completed that mission. Now in the grip of a terminal condition that attacked the spirit as well as the body, I prayed for restored health and a last mission. I prayed for a last mission, but of its nature and character, I hadn't the foggiest idea.

CHAPTER 7

THE LORDS OF HELL

Hold thou the good: define it well;
For fear divine Philosophy
Should push beyond her mark, and be
Procuress to the Lords of Hell.
Alfred, Lord Tennyson (1809-1892) *In Memoriam A.H.H.* (1850), liii

Following the exodus from Egypt, while still en route to the Promised Land, Moses and the children of Israel paused at the border of Edom, a territory inhabited by descendants of Esau. From the threshold of Edom, Moses sent messengers to the king of Edom, saying,

> **". . . Let us pass through thy country. . . we will not turn to the right hand nor to the left, until we have passed thy borders."**

And Edom said unto him,

> **"Thou shalt not pass by me. . . ."**

And the children of Israel said unto him,

> **". . . I will only, without doing any thing else, go through on my feet."**

And he said,

> **"Thou shalt not go through. . . ."**

Thus Edom refused to give Israel passage through his border: wherefore Israel turned away from him.

Numbers 20:14, 17-21 (KJV)

Consider the curious similarity between this passage and the acrimonious denunciation of the scribes and Pharisees, the religious elite of the day, by Jesus of Nazareth more than a thousand years later:

". . . woe unto you, scribes and Pharisees, hypocrites! for ye shut up the kingdom of heaven against men: for ye neither go in yourselves, neither suffer ye them that are entering to go in."
Matthew 23:13 (KJV)

I'd smoothly glided over those words for decades, impervious to any significance deeper than the superficial. Now I saw the account of the Edomite obstruction no longer as history, but as prophecy disguised as history. It was prophecy being fulfilled in a later cycle, well over a thousand years removed, right before the percipient eyes of Jesus of Nazareth . . . and he knew it. The scribes and the pharisaic leadership of that day were, in fact, antitypal Edomites, willfully descended from the earthy hunter Esau, who had sold his birthright for a serving of bread and pottage of lentils.

Edomites were a people who were, for the most part, enemies of the Israelites throughout the annals of history. By the first-century, Edomites were settled in southern Judah as far north as Hebron. It's possible Judas Iscariot, the only non-Galilean among Jesus' handpicked Twelve, may have originally been from Kerioth, located in southern Judah near the Edomite border. If Judas was Edomite by blood as well as temperament, the significance of the Edomite obstruction at the border of the Promised Land swells indeed.

Troglodytic Horites, south and east of the Dead Sea, had originally settled the Edomite homeland. The Hebrew word describing the Horites suggested a people dwelling in caves, holes, cavities, or sockets. That the carnal, earthy Edomites dispossessed such a people to establish their homeland may be part of their typal signature, for post-Constantinian Christianity did just that, taking immediate possession of existing pagan temples and basilicas while launching the construction of many others throughout the Roman Empire.

*

Near all the birds
Will sing at dawn, - and yet we do not take
The chaffering swallow for the holy lark.
Elizabeth Barrett Browning (1806-1861) *Aurora Leigh* (1857), bk. i

"Pharisee" meant something set apart or separated. Their own name for themselves was Hebrew for "companions." Some may have had redeeming potential, despite the blanket condemnation by Jesus of Nazareth. We know that Saul of Tarsus, later known as Paul, the great Christian messenger to the Gentiles, came from their ranks. What appears certain is that as a religious caste, they had evolved to a point where the essentials of their religion had been lost in their acclimatized interpretations. Under their stewardship, service to God had degenerated into a barren, antiseptic formalism. Their message had become carbonized in pride and the ritual observances by which they sheltered themselves, mistaking the appearance of virtue for virtue itself.

The strength of the Pharisees lay in the synagogues, which were found in every town. There has always been a temptation to point to the synagogues as the forerunner of the temple-based homage characteristic of post-Constantinian Christianity. Synagogues, however, while they housed assemblages, were not churches in the modern sense. They were more nearly Jewish community centers used for a variety of activities. It would have been unthinkable at the time for a Jew to admit such a concept as the synagogue structure into any practice considered worship.

The synagogue structure was unknown among Judaism until the advent of the Graeco-Roman conquests of the then known world. There seems to be no reliable historical record or even widely held theory of just how or why synagogue structures came into being at that time. The occupying Romans, although perturbed by the Jews, did not initially attempt to eradicate Judaism. They elected to attempt coexistence with it, giving the Jewish political and religious leadership considerable latitude over determining matters peculiar to the Jewish faith.

The theory suggests synagogue structures were initially introduced, not by the Jews, but by occupying Graeco-Roman armies seeking to capitalize on the Jewish propensity for assemblage. In every community, these structures became a Graeco-Roman Trojan horse, for each had a government tax booth in order to more effectively collect tax revenue from a recalcitrant population. This is the reason the Capernaum centurion built such a structure for the Jews.[20] His affection for the Jews was quite uncharacteristic of a Roman at that time. Perhaps it was related to the forced interface between the two required by what had been his official task, the construction of the synagogue at Capernaum.

Among the many activities carried out at these popular Jewish meeting places, the Mosaic Law was interpreted and studied and fervent prayers were offered for the revival of Israel. Pharisees led these prayers, as they provided the synagogue with its leadership. Under the guidance of the synagogue rulers, whose position was often passed on from father to son, the synagogues were focal points of Jewish community life where tradition was maintained.

* * *

Charlie Gee Penry was sixteen-years-old in the summer of '52. Dwayne and I were as innocent as choirboys compared to Charlie Gee. He took my toys apart to see how they worked, even if – more often than not – he couldn't put them back together, but that peccadillo wasn't his only vice. His active imagination translated into constant lying. Helen Eakins said of her nephew that he would climb a thorn tree to tell a lie when he could sit on the ground and tell the truth; but despite his flaws, Charlie Gee was adventurous, entertaining, and instructive.

Following the war, the Penry brothers' divorced mother and Helen's only sister, Gail, married an ex-Marine. Helen Eakins never warmed up to Harlan Estes. No one other than a preacher, elder, deacon, or song leader of the church marrying her younger sister could've met with her approval.

No one would've ever guessed they were sisters, neither by appearance nor personality. Helen, older by three years, was attractive, but judgmental and straight-laced, almost Puritanical. Gail was beautiful, fun-loving, and engaged in smoking, drinking, and dancing. Helen would occasionally scold Gail over her lifestyle choices, but neither was given to anger. There was never a time during those rare, open disagreements when they were hostile to one another. The two were as close as sisters ever become. They were family.

Harlan Estes was handsome, self-assured and also given to smoking, drinking, and dancing, each a cardinal vice in the eyes of Helen Eakins, although she quietly tolerated the smoking habits of both Chester Eakins and Elijah Roy. Harlan had spent the better part of the war in the brig for falling asleep on guard duty while stationed at a remote Aleutian island outpost. That probably didn't help.

Following their 1946 marriage, Harlan and Gail Estes acquired a modest frame house located in a small subdivision on the outskirts of Osceola. About fifty yards to the east of their house was a deep storm drainage ditch that separated the modest subdivision from the adjacent cotton fields. Such deep, wide ditches with a steep berm on one side were common.

In flat-as-a-table-top Mississippi County, optimal row crop cultivation depended upon both getting rain on the land and promptly getting it off again. When august summer storms patrolled the skies over northeast Arkansas like great galleons upon an immense ocean, these ditches would discharge a torrent of runoff water immediately following their passage. During that brief period of time, there would be rapidly-moving, muddy storm water perhaps six-feet deep and twelve-feet across near ground level. A quarter-mile downstream, the raging flood would disappear into a wide culvert underneath U.S. 61.

Charlie Gee, a skilled autumnal pecan tree thrasher, had located an old cottonwood tree on the bank of the drainage ditch and, climbing out over the chasm, attached a rope to a large lower limb. To the dangling end of this rope, he affixed a piece of deadwood, a crossbar. This allowed him to get a running start on the bank and, holding tightly to the crossbar, swing out over the raging water in a wide circle and return to the bank on the back side of the cottonwood tree, thus completing a thrilling arc of almost three-hundred-sixty degrees. Charlie Gee, Dwayne, and I often made the choice to complete a lesser arc of about two-hundred-seventy degrees and drop directly into the swollen torrent. Surely swimming in storm drainage made one a candidate for polio or typhoid, but we weren't aware of any dangers posed by the drainage ditch, only the great, wide Mississippi River.

* * *

"How can you say,

'We are wise and the law of the Lord is with us'?

Behold, the lying pen of the scribes has made it into a lie. . . .
They have rejected the word of the Lord. What kind of wisdom do they have?" Jeremiah 8:8,9b (NASB)

Scribes belonged to a learned, upper class that served as copyists, editors, and teachers. In times past, such a person controlled the access of the people to the throne room of Kings David and Solomon. However, by the time of Jesus, the scribe was no longer an officer of the court. He'd become a person who interpreted the Scripture, but it's interesting to note that in this capacity, he *still*, most subtly, controlled access to the throne room. A scribe could come from any class or rank, but large numbers of priests were scribes, including Flavius Josephus, the prolific Jewish historian.

The scribes and Pharisees, with few exceptions, came to Jesus only in attempts to discredit him, and he did not carry his message to them uninvited. Because of what the scribes and Pharisees were, because of their obstinacy, he chose to go into the highways and along the hedges to invite guests to his table. When eating and drinking with irreligious Jews and corrupt businessmen, an unthinkable transgression in the eyes of the self-righteous Pharisees, he made this remark in response to their criticism of his actions,

"They that are whole have no need of the physician, but they that are sick: I came not to call the righteous, but sinners to repentance." Mark 2:17b (KJV)

I knew Jesus was speaking metaphorically, that rank sinners, corrupt businessmen and others choosing to live on the fringe, i.e., "they that are sick," were vulnerable to the bad things characteristic of an unsheltered existence, but what application had the phrase, "they that are whole"? The self-righteous, hypocritical Pharisees were not spiritually whole, were they? Jesus was saying that those who *consider themselves* whole, who *consider themselves* healthy in a religious sense are not in need of mending and are, as long as they are in that state, irremediable. It seems you have to hurt first. You have to feel the absence of health, which could be the definition of sickness. Perhaps only then, one has both the need of and the receptiveness to the message of the Great

Physician. Much the same thought was conveyed directly to the Pharisees when they asked,

"Are we blind . . . ?"

Jesus said unto them,

"If ye were blind, ye should have no sin: but now ye say,

'We see';

therefore your sin remaineth." John 9:40b-41 (KJV)

These doctors of the Mosaic Law analyzed the texts, multiplying citations and references, advancing not a single idea without drawing on the Law and the prophets. Jesus departed from the subtleties and trivialities characteristic of the Pharisees, teaching precepts of the Law to which a seeker could respond instinctively. He harbored a distrust of the religious hierarchy, not as much for what they said as for what they did, for what they were, for they valued material success and prestige which assured they could have no unbiased judgment.

* * *

Within a few hours after a storm's passage, the volume of water in the drainage ditch would recede to a trickle. It was during this regression phase of the cycle that Charlie Gee discovered the water moccasin on the slope of the berm, probably driven from its lair by the earlier rapid rise of storm water in the ditch.

The water moccasin is a dangerous semi-aquatic snake that has to be the incarnation of all that is evil. Of all the snakes encountered in my youth, none struck terror into the heart with the same intensity as the feared cottonmouth. Because we lived in the low, swampy flood plain of the Mississippi River and its tributaries, this formidable creature was frequently encountered, occasionally with regrettable results. No encounter with the deadly cottonmouth could ever be described as casual.

The beast was called the "cottonmouth" because of the purity of the white lining of its opened mouth, seen as it launches its strike. It's a pit viper in the same general family as the copperhead and the rattler. The animal grows to an average length of about thirty-inches. It's not the longest snake, but what makes the cottonmouth such a chilling sight is the fact that it's such a stout-bodied snake. Surely its girth-to-length ratio is among the greatest of all snakes, and the triangular shape of its evil head and solid gun-metal gray coloration of its entire body portends its deadly venom and the creature's ready willingness to use it.

* * *

. . . A fool must now and then be right, by chance.
William Cowper (1731-1800) *Conversation*, l.93

In a lifetime of ceremonial homage punctuated by occasional perfunctory Christian service, I was never without modern Edomites, ready and willing to direct me in the modern Christian walk. Misunderstanding is never so compelling as when mixed with truth, no opinion so fatally misleading as one not completely wrong. After all, even a broken watch is right twice a day. Even stock answers occasionally work.

> **". . . your prophets have been like foxes among ruins. You have not gone up into the breaches, nor did you build the wall around the house of Israel to stand in the battle on the day of the LORD. They see falsehood and lying divination who are saying,**
>
> **'The LORD declares,'**
>
> **when the LORD has not sent them; yet they hope for the fulfillment of their word."** Ezekiel 13:4-6 (NASB)

With careful management, every success can hide a multitude of failures. Chester Eakins was a master at it. While in the church, I'd accepted the universal explanation for the inconsistency I saw taking place around me as part of God's mysterious design, a plan that would become clear to me in the hereafter. Feasting at the table spread before me, I'd grown older, sicker, and increasingly impoverished as the words of the prophet were hauntingly realized in real time.

> **It shall even be as when an [sic] hungry man dreameth, and behold, he eateth; but he awaketh, and his soul is empty: or as when a thirsty man dreameth, and behold, he drinketh; but he awaketh, and behold, he is faint, and his soul hath appetite. . . .**
> Isaiah 29:8 (KJV)

* * *

In the bright sunshine and steamy warmth following the passage of a particularly awesome thunderstorm, Dwayne and I spotted Charlie Gee, his head and shoulders visible over the crest of the berm. He was frantically flaying the ground with a garden hoe, alternately pausing and vigorously signaling for us to come. By the time Dwayne and I reached the spot where Charlie Gee was generating such a sweat, he had successfully decapitated the fearsome water moccasin.

While I know the cottonmouth is a creature of God and, unlike certain other species, will not attack a human without provocation, that provocation need only be slight. Its combination of deadly venom and irritable nature made the cottonmouth a target for extermination whenever and wherever it was found. It was, after all, expected. This being the case, there in that hot Mid-South summer sun laid the gory remains of the fully-grown water moccasin, its severed head lying close to its body. But what was most fascinating was the fact that the headless body continued to writhe. It just wouldn't die.

* * *

Paul had sailed to Cyprus on the first leg of what became his first missionary journey. At Paphos, he encountered a Jewish false prophet who opposed their efforts to deliver the Word by invitation to the Roman proconsul, Sergius Paulus, whom Luke described as a "man of intelligence." Paul fixed his gaze upon the false prophet and said,

> **"O full of all subtlety and all mischief, thou child of the devil, thou enemy of all righteousness, wilt thou not cease to pervert the right ways of the Lord?"** Acts 13:10 (KJV)

The harshness Paul used in confronting Bar-jesus – oddly, that ("son of Jesus") was the false prophet's name – is reminiscent of that used by Jesus when addressing the scribes and Pharisees.

> **"Ye serpents, ye generation of vipers, how can ye escape the damnation of hell?"** Matthew 23:33 (KJV)

Confronted with this type of resistance, Jesus and Paul sharply narrowed their attack, throwing courtesy to the wind. Addressing more than the unfeeling words, apathetic deeds, and monumental hypocrisy, they attacked the very person of their antagonist. Shortly before his martyrdom, Stephen's implacable response before the august Jewish Sanhedrin, composed as it was of this same class of religious champion, was . . .

> **"Ye stiffnecked and uncircumcised in heart and ears, ye do always resist the Holy Ghost; as your fathers did, so do ye."**
> Acts 7:51 (KJV)

Full of deceit, full of fraud, enemies of righteousness, serpents, brood of vipers, stiffnecked, uncircumcised in heart and ears (i.e., spiritually unclean), hypocrites, children of the devil – all these were expressions used against this religious elite. Unless you're familiar with just how seriously the pious Jew took these particular expressions, it's easy to underestimate the magnitude of the insult. Yet there was never a time when Jesus, John the Baptist, Stephen, or the apostle Paul equivocated when confronted with the false teacher.

With words such as these, any possibility of reconciliation was foreclosed. These four all willingly and deliberately embarked upon a course of open warfare against the most powerful, influential and spiritually-minded element of the contemporary religious establishment.

I didn't miss the subtle point, easily overlooked amid these outpourings of indignation by Jesus and these giants of the faith: in every instance, the object of their wrath was neither the idol-worshiping pagan nor the backsliding Jew. It was instead a class indigenous to the faith, a class that would today be composed, not of robbers and murderers or even of Sunday couch potatoes or golfing enthusiasts, but of active churchmen, even the pillars of the Church. It seems the enemy inflicting the most grievous damage always presents in the guise of a friend, accomplishing the final betrayal with a brotherly kiss.

So clomb this first grand thief into God's fold:
So since into his church lewd hirelings climb.
Thence up he flew, and on the tree of life,
The middle tree and the highest there than grew,
Sat like a cormorant.
John Milton (1608-1674) *Paradise Lost* (1667), 1668 ed. bk. iv, l.192

I knew my translated copy of the Bible had embedded within its pages a handful of critically deceptive biases arising from concepts determined sacred *ex post facto*. I knew these concepts were neither taught nor practiced by the earliest Christians. What I didn't immediately appreciate was that the living, breathing assembly of the Church had among its leadership those who would fiercely embrace and defend these immigrant concepts. In doing so, they would relegate to *de facto* second-class status the weightier provisions of their faith, offering with their "good news" precepts and traditions that had evolved long after the fact.

> **"O my people, they which lead thee cause thee to err and destroy the way of thy paths."** Isaiah 3:12b (KJV)

The observation reflects upon some successfully entrenched as messengers of Jesus, considered angels of light and servants of righteousness by the unsuspecting flock sustaining them.

> **. . . such are false apostles, deceitful workers, transforming themselves into the apostles of Christ. And no marvel; for Satan himself is transformed into an angel of light. Therefore it is no great thing if his ministers also be transformed as the ministers of righteousness. . . .** 2 Corinthians 11:13-15a (KJV)

To this day, I remain haunted by the question. Tell me if you know the answer. If not the mercenary Elmer Gantrys who've polished their act, eagerly employing expensive, high-tech marketing techniques that make their crusade as effective as a two-hundred-mile-long drift net, exactly who are the modern day ministers of Satan disguised as ministers of righteousness? Who are the modern equivalents of the scribes and Pharisees?

The spirit of the scribes and Pharisees was not an isolated phenomenon. That spirit continues to be pandemic among those claiming to seek and follow God, whether Jew or Gentile, Catholic or Protestant, traditional or evangelical. There were impenitent scribes and Pharisees in Jesus' day; false apostles, false prophets and false teachers in Paul's day; antichrists in John's day; and false prophets in Revelation's apocalyptic pronunciations. All have had a common bond – all present themselves as representative of divine authority. All present themselves as coming in the name of the Lord.

"Therefore, behold, I am against the prophets,"

declares the LORD,

'who steal My words from each other. Behold, I am against the prophets . . . who use their tongues and declare,

"The Lord declares."

'Behold, I am against those who have prophesied false dreams . . . and related them, and led My people astray by their falsehoods and reckless boasting; yet I did not send them or command them, nor do they furnish this people the slightest benefit,'

declares the LORD." Jeremiah 23:30-32 (NASB)

The question cries out for an answer. Who are the latter day scribes and Pharisees, false messengers and teachers? Dared I honestly think modern man had reached a level of sophistication and enlightenment that foreclosed the opportunity for such a ubiquitous class? What modern man may have reached is the near zenith of sophistry and benightedness that absolutely guarantees their thriving existence.

The scribes and Pharisees were experts in the Scripture and the self-appointed holiest class of worshiper. If they condemned the Messiah and his teachings at his first visitation, who can be expected to resist him most vigorously in the season of his Second Coming? The prostitutes and corrupt businessmen with whom he openly ate and drank? The theory holds otherwise.

*

Those currently indifferent to or at war with God and the Bible find contemporary religion at best an incomprehensible puzzle and at worst a sham. How was Jesus able to communicate so readily with such individuals? How was it the religious outcasts of his day responded to him, seeking him out, inviting him into their ostracized communities, eager to hear more of what he had to say? More importantly, why was it he accepted these opportunities, avoiding the pointed discussions of the scribes and Pharisees that he had found so engaging in his youth?

The theory submits the messianic mission was never to the religious elite, but to the outcast and disenfranchised of that set – as he became. To the thief on the cross[21] and the publican who went up to the Temple to pray[22], Jesus held out a spectacular olive branch of peace. This was no less than the New Testament promised land, the long-awaited, much anticipated kingdom of God in real time, *completely bypassing the established, institutionalized religiosity of the day.*

The rank sinners and outcasts of first-century religiosity took no offense in what he said or what he did or what he was. They neither take offense in him today nor will they do so at his Second Coming. They're offended by the modern expression of Christianity.

Although not one of them, Jesus went in and out among those paying the price of misguidance, pointedly avoiding those who had sold out to misguidance. The former received him and his message, which admonished them to continue no more in their past practices, but to turn to the true God, lest even worse things happen to them in a land where time and chance affected them all. These were not individuals who had egocentric and/or economic reason to resist his message. It was the religious leadership and the industry dependent craftsmen who considered him and his message a threat. They were, of course, correct. His message was a threat to their frame world. It still is.

* * *

Charlie Gee, Dwayne, and I hunkered down in the hot sun, sweat running down our foreheads and dripping off our noses, marveling at the curious scene. The snake's severed head was lying there, still and lifeless, just as expected, but the evil, ominous body of the beast continued to twist with a motion similar to that of a sidewinder. It wasn't going anywhere, but it was in continual motion.

Now the death response of barnyard animals was not unfamiliar to me. I'd often witnessed Lila Roy corral a couple of barnyard chickens and carry the pinioned birds to the chopping block, right hand swinging a hatchet, left hand solidly gripping four chicken feet, the wings of both birds fully extended by gravity. Once positioned at the block, she would dispatch both birds – one at a time, of course – with a single stroke of the hatchet, but the surreal part of the ritual was yet to come.

For a few moments following the decapitation, the headless bodies of the chickens would flail around the barnyard, their wings flapping and legs extending as though they were attempting to get airborne. There was, of course, no coordination to these responses. The grotesque dance would slow and finally end, all within about thirty to forty-five seconds. The carcasses of the unfortunate birds were then dipped in boiling water, plucked, gutted, singed and cut up for the frying pan.

The fact that the snake's body continued to writhe after the head was severed was not entirely unfamiliar. What was alien was the fact that this motion just wouldn't stop. Seconds turned into minutes. Minutes turned into a quarter-hour, and still there was no cessation of the residual movement of the snake's body.

In the end, the ever-inquisitive Charlie Gee moved to autopsy the still-moving carcass. With his pocket knife – which all sixteen-year-olds carried, the same as their fathers and grandfathers – he carefully approached the still-moving body. What I witnessed next burned its way into my memory where it has remained ever since.

***

Such as for their bellies' sake,
Creep and intrude, and climb into the fold.
Of other care they little reckoning make,
Than how to scramble at the shearers' feast,
And shove away the worthy bidden guest.
Blind mouths! that scarce themselves know how to hold
A sheep-hook, or have learn'd aught else the least
That to the faithful herdman's art belongs!
John Milton (1608-1674) *Lycidas* (1637), l.114

Jude understood the cycles in prophetic history and recognized the antitypes of false messengers from over a thousand years earlier as being present in the midst of the first-century gatherings. He warned of certain persons "written about long before" as having crept in and for pay rushed headlong into the error of Balaam, i.e., the selling of the people of God for monetary gain. Jude identified these persons as being in attendance at first-century feasts, effectively early observances of the Lord's Supper.[23] Writing in the same era as Jude, Peter spoke of the rise of false messengers who in greed exploited the people with false words, having forsaken the right way.[24] Lastly, in the book of Revelation, the risen Christ acknowledged among the assemblage at Pergamum some who held to the teachings of Balaam.[25]

> **The Lord enters into judgment with the elders and princes of his people,**
>
> > **"It is you who have devoured the vineyard; the plunder of the poor is in your houses."** Isaiah 3:14 (NASB)

The "error of Balaam," the "way of Balaam," and the "teaching of Balaam" are phrases in the ancient record describing an attitude of the heart. It's a rationalization whereby purported servants of God can, at least according to their own way of thinking, achieve the dual purposes of both God and man. This marketing of the promise brings spiritual "death" both to the prophet and the people. The manifestation of this spiritual "death" is visible in their living outside the promised protection of God, in a land where bad things happen to supposedly good people.

> **For the sins of her prophets and the iniquities of her priests . . . they . . . wandered as blind men in the streets. . . .**
>
> Lamentations 4:13-14 (KJV)

In addressing this caste of religious leader, Peter confirmed the agency of cycles when looking to the history of those drawn to God, saying,

> **. . . there were false prophets also among the people, even as there shall be false teachers among you. . . . And many shall follow their pernicious ways; by reason of whom the way of truth shall be evil spoken of. And through covetousness shall they with feigned words make merchandise of you. . . .**
>
> 2 Peter 2:1-3a (KJV)

Paul said this class of religious leader within the assemblies professed to know God, but by their deeds, they denied God.

> **Your iniquities have turned away these things, and your sins have withholden good things from you. For among my people are . . . wicked men: they lay wait, as he that setteth . . . a trap, they catch men. . . . their houses full of deceit . . . they overpass the deeds of the wicked: they judge not . . . the cause of the fatherless, yet they prosper; and the right of the needy do they not judge.** Jeremiah 5:23-28 (KJV)

What constitutes the "houses full of deceit" if not the modern temples of worship they are so industrious in initiating. As some of these may be horrified at hearing their Christianity doubted, so would they be similarly horrified at seeing early Christianity practiced.[26]

*

It has never been a characteristic of one socially and politically astute to make observations such as these and suggest they have parallel complement in modern Christianity. It may be impolitic, but it is necessary, for the theory holds those within the modern Church who proclaim peace (wellness) and freedom in their message are themselves most enslaved by that which they promote and allow. There are none more enslaved than those who falsely believe they are free. But opportunism will always arise to exploit the potential for gain. It is, after all, a characteristic of success. Success will make fools admired and villains honest, and – God knows – America loves a success.

The message of Jesus of Nazareth, undiluted by time and cultural evolution, was neither designed nor expected to transform society in general, but individuals in specific. For those with hearts and souls given to social, cultural and political revolution – and they are many – this is *anathema*, but such ambition has the capacity to plunge the pilgrim and the flock into a narcotic sleep of misdirection. St. Augustine noted that out of the will proceeds desire; and out of desire, habit; and out of habit, necessity. As long as habit is fed, the victim sleeps in oblivion. Anesthetized to the especial nature of the message and dependent upon culture and tradition, such an individual will have little or nothing to put in its place in the day of the east wind.[27] But that, too, is another story for another time.

*

Visibly alienated, secular opportunists are, for the most part, up-front people like Chester Eakins and Jody Tremain. They're comfortable with who and what they are. Their lot may be with the thief on the cross, but he at least gained favor as one coming at the eleventh hour. These still have hope. Modern religion's outcasts may be closer today to the kingdom of God than the well-meaning, but mis-guided communicant engaged in impotent ceremonial worship behind a walled structure that, despite its ostensibly proffered welcome mat, is effectively a fortified city, a palace of strangers unacknowledged by God.

* * *

Charlie Gee swiftly and surgically opened the writhing body of the cottonmouth. In a few short seconds, there before our wide eyes was the explanation for the continual motion of the snake's body. On the ground amidst the mud and the bloodied remains of the now immobile snake carcass were several small, round, membranous sacs . . . and they were moving. The membrane comprising the sac was transparent, at least enough to identify the evil that was within. And that which was within each sac was a single, curled-up embryonic water moccasin. And we had strewn these sacs like dragon's teeth upon the ground around us, unaware they were soon to sprout up as armed and hostile combatants.

* * *

> **. . ."Pasture the flock doomed to slaughter. Those who buy them, slay them and go unpunished, and each of those who sell them says,**
>
> **'Blessed be the Lord, for I have become rich!'**
>
> **And their own shepherds have no pity on them."**
>
> Zechariah 11:4-5 (NASB)

The question of which came first, derelict leadership or vapid laity is not dissimilar to that of the chicken and the egg. There's evidence incriminating both. But when viewing the world from the bottom of the ditch, the point becomes moot. Jesus was surely determined to erase the barren, unproductive conformity of the Pharisees from men's hearts and instill the importance of deeds motivated by character.

Who is the happy Warrior? Who is he
That every man in arms should wish to be?
It is the generous spirit, who, when brought
Among the tasks of real life, hath wrought
Upon the plan that pleased his childish thought:
Whose high endeavours are an inward light
That makes the path before him always bright:
Who, with a natural instinct to discern
What knowledge can perform, is diligent to learn.

William Wordsworth (1770-1850) *Character of the Happy Warrior* (1807)

I dared not advance by rising early on Sunday morning and attending the Sunday school and worship services of the Church. If enjoying that particular activity and/or delivering (or receiving) some benefit therefrom, I was by all means free to do so, but that wouldn't produce a solution to the problem. It couldn't because that activity is offspring of the model that left me in the ditch in the first place. The theory suggests regular attendance and tithing to the temple-based operation change nothing. Far from demonstrating the heart of flesh, this action can quite capably mask the heart of stone.

* * *

Charlie Gee proceeded with the ultimate step of his assault on the evil before us. He slit open each of the small membranous sacs, and in a few moments, the embryonic cottonmouths were released.

If you're inclined to think the offspring of the cottonmouth to be cute, innocent little things like puppies or kittens seeking the comfort of a mother's teat, you'd be mistaken. These came into the world scurrying and aggressively defending their self-interest. As the teeth sown by Cadmus, they sprang up, getting in each other's way to fight.

It was a bizarre sight. These tiny little snakes, about the size of a standard kitchen matchstick and, except for their coloration, perfect miniatures of the dark, foreboding evil that had spawned them, had their tiny fangs bared as they instinctively fought for their survival. That most feared characteristic – that evil temperament directed at any attacker, real or imagined – was not taught them by their mother or their clan. They were born with it.

Before we left the berm late that afternoon in the summer of '52, Charlie Gee had killed them all. It was, after all, expected.

* * *

Solitudinem faciunt pacem appellant.
They make a wilderness and call it peace.
Tacitus (55 or 56 - ca.120 C.E.) *Agricola*, 30

Jesus said false teachers would be identifiable "by their fruits." So what are the fruits of the priest, pastor, preacher, or minister and his flock? Are they justice, mercy, and righteousness (equitable conduct) flowing down like a river? Or are they brick and mortar, carpeted aisles and altars, cushioned pews, stained glass windows, ornate foyers, lavishly bedecked choirs, and staggering debt service, maintenance, and staffing obligations – and all of this sprinkled with benevolent and missionary service as dried onion and chives on an otherwise bland baked potato? Missionary and benevolent endeavors, the only legitimate enterprises of the assembly, are thereby effectively transformed into temple and priesthood.

How fast has brother followed brother,
From sunshine to the sunless land!
William Wordsworth (1770-1850) *Extempore Effusion upon the Death of James Hogg* (1835)

What injustice did those who went before us find in God, that they went far from him to walk after things vain, futile and empty? By intent or misunderstanding, those in whom I'd had confidence had never exposed the misconceptions responsible for the shadowy, late-twentieth-century captivity wherein I had found myself constrained.

> **. . . the Lord has rejected those in whom you trust . . . you shall not prosper with them. . . .** Jeremiah 2:37b (NASB)

> **Your prophets . . . have not exposed your iniquity so as to restore you from captivity, but they have seen for you false and misleading oracles. . . .** Lamentations 2:14 (NASB)

> **. . . . from the least of them even to the greatest of them, everyone is greedy for gain, and from the prophet even to the priest, everyone deals falsely. They have healed the brokenness of My people superficially, saying,**
>
> **'Peace, peace,'**
>
> **but there is no peace."** Jeremiah 6:13-14 (NASB)

The apostle Paul observed,

> **. . . in the last days difficult times will come. . . . men will be lovers of self, lovers of money . . . lovers of pleasure rather than lovers of God; holding to a form of godliness . . . avoid such men as these.** 2 Timothy 3:1-5 (NASB)

These are not the openly ungodly. They are not the disenfranchised unchurched. These whom Paul advised Timothy to avoid wear the cloak of godliness. These arise from within the body of those ostensibly Christian. As the Edomites, they neither enter nor allow those who would enter to go in, but assign them to make their way in a sterile world where bad things happen, as likely as not, to good people.

Why had my late-twentieth-century Christianity walk been so bewildering? Unless I willed it so, the answer wasn't in the watered-down excuses ecclesiastically proffered for God's failure to live up to my expectations. There's never been a time in history when a people in communal relationship with God had to sit in bewilderment and confess there were misfortunes beyond their understanding with no person of God to declare an answer. This became a post-Constantinian phenomenon when worship evolved from the effectual into the institutional.

*

The Church – local, regional, and global – has both power and the will to use it, but she's quite content to live and let live, a protected, patronized giant amidst the corporate jungle of world commerce. Allow her necessary space, don't menace her, and she'll be unconcerned with you. But sensing a credible threat, her courtiers will emerge in an attack mode that's instinctive.

Jesus' public condemnation of the scribes and Pharisees and his succinct, pointed defense at his pre-dawn mock trial struck a blow to the head of prevailing religiosity, those whom he'd described as vipers. But the prophets have always shocked the religious by their blasphemous attitude toward religion. And it was for blasphemy that the intemperate offspring of institutionalized religion demanded and received his death by crucifixion.

* * *

I stiffened slightly in the pale gold recliner, alert again to my surroundings. Something had changed. Carefully, I checked one-by-one the semaphoric markers that had guided me to that anchorage. Yes, that was it. The refrigerator had shut down and was now silent. The old Pekinese had quietly moved across the thick carpet to the cool tile of the foyer, far beyond the range where I could hear his soft, sonorous snoring.

My eyes studied the room that had become my citadel, recording everything there was to see in minute detail. There was the discordant array of family snapshots and photographs on the fireplace mantle; Anna's potted, late summer greenery on the hearth; and the bookcase against the east wall, crowded with more pictures and memorabilia than books. Among the muddle collected there was the third place trophy I'd struggled to win just two years before in a club racquetball tournament.

Even then I was sick, but failing to suspect the condition, I couldn't respond to it. Mistaking the signals the condition was giving me every time I took to the court, I accepted the medical diagnosis of deconditioning as the cause of my increasing on-court difficulty. I relentlessly practiced harder and harder, spending more and more time on the court, employing mechanical devices to brace the weakening knees and ankles. I tried various combinations of glove, powder, and tape to augment the flagging grip of my racquet hand. I believed that what the weak, deconditioned body needed most was more and more exercise and conditioning. If fact, what it so desperately needed was a cessation of all such activity and major surgical intervention – just as my experience was trying to tell me.

My eyes continued their one-hundred-eighty degree scan, registering the soft leather chair diagonally across the room; the group family portrait on the south wall, flanked by the individual portraits of Anna and me; and the long, white divan close to my right hand, adorned with Anna's handmade Afghans. I'd seen all this every day for years, but now I pondered each and every object as time stretched and extended like some unreal rubber band.

The physician eventually responsible for my correct diagnosis had told me. Soon, very soon, we would have to make a decision whether to act now to annul the beast while I still possessed the strength to survive the ordeal or else wait for the certain conclusion. He'd said the surgery was complicated and "presented many opportunities for something to go wrong." It involved immediate, grievous risk and enormous expense. Only a qualified recovery was likely, and that by no means certain. It was in the truest sense a last-ditch procedure, an operation that would never be performed on anyone with a chance of living otherwise, but it couldn't be attempted if you waited too long. To wait too long was to allow the beast to sap the body's strength beyond its ability to survive such an operation. It was unbearable to commit too soon, and you dared not wait too late. It was a fine line.

*

It was half-past-ten and the children at the school had ceased their play. I was anticipating the dissonance when I heard the station wagon ease into the driveway. The car door slammed shut and in a few short moments, I heard the sound of Anna's keys rattling outside the front door.

Does the road wind up-hill all the way?
Yes, to the very end.
Will the day's journey take the whole long day?
From morn to night, my friend.
Christina Rossetti (1830-1894) *Up-Hill*

*

There was a short burst from a car horn out front. Anna went to the door and waved. Within seconds, the cab driver opened the glass storm door and took in both hands the suitcases Anna had placed in the foyer. Jared had arrived a few minutes ago with Rebekah and stood at the door beside his sister.

Anna approached my chair and smiled warmly, informing me it was time for us to go. She stood there silently, patiently, her hands clasped in front of her, smiling expectantly.

Refreshed in the half-hour since Anna arrived home and comfortable once more in the faded gold recliner beside my window on the world, I glanced around the room one last time. It was the room that had been my sanctuary, my enclave, the room where I'd revisited scenes of my childhood.

I glanced out the sliding glass door that led out onto the wooden deck and the modest, trim backyard. I scanned the carefully mowed, shaded grounds of Immaculate Conception Catholic Church and Sarah Barnhill Elementary School. I mentally registered the available sunlight, still diffused by the heavy cloud cover, took a deep breath, and gave one last look to Anna.

She was still standing there, hands folded patiently in front of her, smiling expectantly, waiting for my reply as though she would wait forever. Releasing a deep breath in a long sigh, I nodded my head and pushed up from the pale gold recliner. Anna responded instantly, taking me by the arm with both hands and guiding me to my feet. I turned my back on what had been my window on the world and on the enclave with which I'd become so familiar, where in solitude I had been least alone. With effort as much mental as physical, I crossed the room. I hugged the children at the doorway, telling each good-bye. Then it was time to go.

CHAPTER 8

A LOFTIER RACE

These things shall be! A loftier race
Than e'er the world hath known shall rise,
With flame of freedom in their souls,
And light of knowledge in their eyes.
John Addington Symonds (1840-1893) *Hymn*

As nineteenth-century livestock, we are indelibly branded in our early youth with the mark of the clan. The most open-minded are not perfectly free of indigenous bias, even when convicted by reason. Thus, even for those who conquer the difficult immediately, the inconceivable may take some time, for the theory beckons a Copernican revolution, suggesting the god of modern mainstream Christianity isn't God at all, but a culturally-forged, tilted projection of God. This heretofore unthinkable conclusion is the wellspring from which answers to thorny theological questions spill like water over a dam.

At the still point of the turning world.
Neither flesh nor fleshless;
Neither from nor towards;
at the still point, there the dance is,
But neither arrest nor movement.
T. S. Eliot (1888-1965) *Four Quartets. Burnt Norton*, 2

The theory holds the first-century model was divinely designed to be the still point of the turning world, an ultimate solution. The assembly of adherents was to grow by divine addition, just as did the neophyte Christian movement in Jerusalem, but the paradigm was born full grown, as ancient at birth as it will be at Judgment.

The evidence lies in the unclaimed blessings of Deuteronomy 28. They had accumulated around me for decades, first as a youthful acolyte, then as an active churchman-in-good-standing, and lastly as a self-exiled constituent of the vast, inaudible unchurched-in-America. I'd never been able to see it, neither from within the palace walls nor while huddled outside, shadowed by its immense silhouette. I may never have seen it except for the condition and, in its aftermath, the liberating splendor of that willingness to step away from the linear alignment along which all the varied manifestations of the modern Church are positioned.

* * *

Pittsburgh, Allegheny County, Pennsylvania
September, 1988

The third-floor, private accommodations at "Presby" Hospital were spacious, but emotionally sterile. My medical insurance was paying for a semiprivate room, the only accommodations available on 10-B, but I had resisted the notion of spending that night on 10-B and, to my surprise, the front desk had accommodated me.

Nobody was demanding their money immediately anyway, at least not in my case. The medical insurance had been sufficient to get me admitted. Without it, the hospital's business office would've required the up-front cash equivalent of two-and-one-half-times my annual salary prior to granting admission, and my annual salary was respectable. I'd have to figure out how to pay my share later, but I couldn't stay on 10-B that night.

* * *

> **. . . in my thirst they gave me vinegar to drink. Let their table become a snare before them: and that which should have been for their welfare, let it become a trap. Let their eyes be darkened, that they see not. . . .** Psalms 69:21-23 (KJV)

In my modern Christian walk, I'd experienced bewilderment, disappointment, confusion, and frustration. When it came to answers, I'd first been conditioned and then, in turn, conditioned others to look inward for what must be either their own personal failings or else the honorable testing of their stalwart faith by a sovereign God. In so doing, I'd first received and then, in ignorance, dispensed the vinegar offered to Jesus at the cross.

. . ."Oh my Lord, if the LORD be with us, why then is all this befallen us? and where be all his miracles which our fathers told us of. . . ." Judges 6:13a (KJV)

Because of misunderstanding and misdirection, I had been reaching out for that which I knew in my heart my latter day fathers-in-the-faith had spent entire lifetimes seeking without grasping, claiming without experiencing.

* * *

Some well-meaning soul had made an attempt to add color to the surroundings of my third-floor hospital room by positioning a mural of some cryptographic orange-brown swirl on the wall opposite the bed, but I thought the effort largely wasted. A Gideon Bible neatly placed at an angle to the corner of the dresser top and a small box of white facial tissue on the night stand were the only items in that room emitting so much as a trace of human warmth. The only window opened onto the bare, gray walls of an immediately proximate building a few feet across a narrow alleyway.

I stood before that window and glazed two floors below to a flat tar-and-gravel roof where someone's lunch wrappings swirled endlessly in the vortex created by the canyon of stone. I looked upward and could see nine more stories of the adjoining building, but I couldn't see the leaden sky. Only gray light filtering through a gray overcast and reflecting off that gray stone building exterior entered my window.

On one of the windows across the chasm, high above me, white adhesive tape affixed to the inside of the glass formed large, slightly crooked letters that clearly read, GOD HELP ME. I thought to myself that some poor soul went to a lot of trouble to spell that backwards from the inside.

For brief periods during the twenty-day protocol evaluation that followed, I sat before that hospital room window with its stark depiction of a cold, hard world without warmth. From the pale gold recliner, I could observe the sights and sounds of life beyond the sliding glass door. There were squirrels and field rabbits occasionally appearing in the yard, a resident chipmunk and a family of redbirds visiting the redwood deck, and the delightful sounds of the children at play on the grounds of the school a few score yards away through the well-spaced trees. From the hospital room where I found myself that late September, the view was cold and foreboding.

* * *

Obtruding false rules pranked in reason's garb.

John Milton (1608-1674) *Comus* (1634), l.759

An institutionalized infrastructure, varied sacramental rites, building funds, trendy programs and activities – all of these so agreeably constitute the marrow of modern mainstream Christianity. If they were displaced from the creedal framework of the contemporary Christian mind, would there be anything to fill the vacuum? These things are, after all, a necessity to those who love and have staked their well-being upon the evolutionary model. But to the Christian expatriate who would enter in upon the New Testament kingdom of God, the anticipated void is a ghost, a banshee, a figment of now formidable post-fourth-century Christian imaginings. Anything else is certain to fail – again. Any further evolutionary refinement of the model, regardless of motive, formula or label, will constitute neither nativity nor reformation, but only another new and wearisome "church." However, *replace* the model and the fearful void becomes instead pure, undiluted Christian veneration of God by means of service, missionary and benevolent, to mankind.

The theory suggests this model, the still point paradigm, is even now realizable for the few so electing it, and by complex, confusing, and contradictory modern canonical standards, its simplistic parameters are simply breathtaking.

* * *

I don't know how he learned of me or secured my name and location. I'd been in residence at Presby Hospital only a day or two when he came down from 10-B and, without invitation or appointment, entered my third-floor room. He was a young man with dark hair and features that betrayed his tramontane ancestry. Although he was only weeks out from the surgery I'd soon face, I would never have guessed it if he hadn't told me. He both looked and acted that whole, that well.

Of Chilean parentage, he was American born and raised. An outspoken Christian, he was young enough to be a son, possessing all the vitality and enthusiasm the young so often bring to their Christian commitment. He said he had survived the surgery so he could become a missionary. At a point in our conversation, he asked if he could pray for me. Of course, I acceded and he appealed to God, right then and there, for my health and welfare in a manner and tone consistent with our brief exchange.

I was to spend the next ten weeks in his close company, never suspecting when and how our relationship would end

* * *

So many gods, so many creeds,
So many paths that wind and wind,
While just the art of being kind
Is all the sad world needs.
Ella Wheeler Wilcox (1855-1919) *The World's Need*

Think about it. In its apparent weakness lies its phenomenal strength. It has no legal identity, no distinctive denominational name for the assembly or for the individual, beyond that of learner or disciple. It has no label for its principles other than the way of Jesus. It owns no real estate and no personal property. It has no address and no telephone number other than those of the individual communicants. There's no web site, no way to solicit it, target it, use it, or abuse it. There's no way to sell anything to it or buy anything from it, no way to make money off of it or out of it. There's no indiscriminate proselytism and, in fact, no membership except that based upon demonstrated character that in word and deed reflects the way of Jesus of Nazareth. There's no way to hide or become lost within it. There's no payroll, no mortgage, no bonds to retire, and no bills to pay. It is the body of the called (out) of God bared to the heart, absent every layered aggrandizement that has resulted in the modern facade of the Church.

The proposition needn't be alarming. Those discouragingly-churched, the unchurched, and the never-churched don't have any great material and/or psychological stake in modern mainstream Christianity. The concept was hardly alarming to those with whom Jesus of Nazareth was most often found eating and drinking. It was not alarming to the rank-and-file of Jewish and pagan disposition at the time. Only among those who became increasingly well-placed in the ecclesiastical structure and/or economically dependent upon the Church as an industry did it become progressively difficult to consider and embrace the concepts of Jesus. Perhaps that is why the apostle Paul was to observe,

> **. . . ye see . . . brethren, how that not many wise . . . not many mighty, not many noble, are called. . . .** 1 Corinthians 1:26 (KJV)

*

There had always been resident in my psyche a respect which made me reluctant to question anyone or anything wrapped in the cloak of the Church. The term and the model it describes are sacrosanct, but so impregnated with alien notions that first-century Christians living and working in a modern environment might do well to surrender the use of the term as well as the model. Do not misunderstand. There's nothing inherently wrong with the word "church." It's simply already taken.

* * *

I'd been in the hospital twenty days and my condition was continuing to deteriorate. Twenty minutes a day in the stiff, vinyl chair by the window was all I could manage. The gripping despair that fatigue and confusion can create in the mind of one who has defined his existence by the power of his concentration and analytical ability was overwhelming. The familiar supports to the frame and substance of my world were slipping away, like sand through an hourglass.

I thought I'd hidden it well at first. I know I'd worked at hiding it well. A few minutes a day under a sun lamp, creating a facial suntan that masked the jaundiced complexion; tinted eyeglasses to conceal the yellowing in the whites of the eyes; prescription medicines to control the fortunately mild edema – all these I had employed, yet those who knew me well could tell.

The doctor responsible for my ultimate diagnosis had said I could possibly live another year if not for the dangerous unpredictable and uncontrollable variceal hemorrhaging. The odds of surviving a major variceal hemorrhage were about even, making it one of the most formidable crises in medicine. I'd survived three increasingly severe hemorrhages, the last having been quite desperate. I surely wouldn't survive a fourth.

* * *

To work a wonder, God would have her shown,
At once, a bud, and yet a rose full-blown.
Robert Herrick (1591-1674) *The Virgin Mary*

For the first few generations, early Christian communities exhibited great variety and remarkable numerical growth in the absence of a centralized organization and structure. Perhaps the closest thing to such a structure was the respect the new Christian communities showed for the admonitions of the Jerusalem leadership, after the pattern shown for the Jewish authorities in Jerusalem by the communities of the Diaspora. This, however, never developed into administrative machinery for extensive oversight.

In this glaring absence of central governance lies the divine genius. The first-century model, with Christianity a movement and not an institution, was a pure service model. This was not service that manifested itself as a periodic project of the group, service merely complementary to the modern mainstream Church experience. It was service which, as background radiation, pervaded the consciousness and consumed all of the dedicated resources of the assembly, both of time and money. It was service first to the needs of one's immediate family, secondly to the individual needs of the community of committed votaries of Jesus, and lastly to the missionary and benevolence needs of the family of man. It was service in that order and as opportunity presented itself, mindful of the Pauline sanction of sensitivity to such opportunity.

. . . ye have well done, that ye did communicate with my affliction. Philippians 4:14 (KJV)

But the still point paradigm soon bore the indelible impress of the political framework within which it had arisen. So deeply did the Roman Empire place its stamp on the evolutionary Church that to this day, the fragments into which it has broken have preserved those features, especially those of outward organization. The largest fragment, the Roman Catholic Church, in many ways perpetuates the remarkable genius that was pre-Christian Rome.

* * *

It's an early October morning in an unfamiliar city hundreds of miles from home. I sit at the small breakfast table in Anna's cramped second-floor apartment ten blocks from Presby Hospital. I've been permitted leave from the hospital provided I remain in the immediate vicinity and wear at all times the pager issued to me by hospital personnel.

The Pittsburgh weather has changed for the better. Warm, bright morning sunlight christens the small dinette table. Just big enough for two, it sits nestled against a window overlooking the shaded lawn of the manor-turned-multi-unit-apartment house.

The call had come late last evening. My surgery is scheduled for later this afternoon or early this evening. The hospital wants me to return as soon as possible.

I look out from an elevation of perhaps twelve to fifteen feet at the golden autumn of '88, mesmerized by the leaves which fall like confetti outside this third and last window on the world.

Now it is autumn and the falling fruit
and the long journey towards oblivion . . .
Have you built your ship of death,
O have you?
D. H. Lawrence (1885-1930) *The Ship of Death*

* * *

After the dramatic incident on Mount Carmel when Elijah humiliated the four-hundred-fifty prophets of Baal, he fled before Jezebel, wife of King Ahab, who had sworn to kill him in revenge. In his fatigue, he rested under a juniper tree and requested for himself that he might die. But he didn't die. An angel of the Lord came to him, giving him spiritual food and drink to strengthen him. And he went in the strength of that food and drink forty days and forty nights to the mountain of God. There he took refuge in a cleft in the rock. The Lord came to him there and Elijah responded,

> **. . ."I have been very jealous for the LORD God of hosts: because the children of Israel have forsaken thy covenant, thrown down thine altars, and slain thy prophets with the sword; and I, even I only, am left; and they seek my life, to take it away."**
> 1 Kings 19:10 (KJV)

Elijah was told to stand on the mountain before the Lord, and God displayed to Elijah exactly where his great strength was to be found.

> **. . . and, behold, the LORD passed by, and a great and strong wind rent the mountains, and brake in pieces the rocks before the LORD; but the LORD was not in the wind: and after the wind an earthquake; but the LORD was not in the earthquake: and after the earthquake a fire; but the LORD was not in the fire: and after the fire a still, small voice. The Lord said to Elijah,**
>
> > **"I have left . . . seven thousand in Israel . . . which have not bowed unto Baal. . . ."** 1 Kings 19:11-18 (KJV)

Seven-thousand, if literal, may have been less than one-percent of the total adult male population of Israel at the time, but it would be enough. And Elijah was not alone.

* * *

A magnificent orchestration had begun at Presby, something roughly akin to the countdown to a shuttle launch. Highly trained professionals were at that moment progressing through a well-planned checklist. Soon, a four-man team of surgeons would commit to what would be a thirteen-hour operation, about average. The medical team would surgically exorcise the sinister evil that had been at work within me all these many years, perhaps since birth. Silently and stealthily, the beast had insidiously robbed me of youth and vigor without my realizing it, leaving me believing my struggle and distress was all part of the natural process of living and dying. So subtle were the symptoms, so well-disguised in the give and take of everyday life that even the medical experts had consistently failed to respond to what was becoming increasingly evident. The condition that had been casually draining away my life was that unexpected.

Having exorcised that which had been rendered increasingly ineffectual by the contrivance of the beast, my redemption would hardly be concluded. There would remain the need to replace that which had been rendered useless and dysfunctional with that which was wholesome and serviceable.

* * *

There was a time in the history of God's people when Israel was brought low because of the Midianites, and the sons of Israel cried out to the Lord. The Lord spoke to them through a prophet.

> **"I brought you up from Egypt, and brought you forth out of the house of bondage; and I delivered you out of the hand of the Egyptians, and out of the hand of all that oppressed you, and drave them out from before you, and gave you their land; and I said unto you,**
>
> > **'I am the LORD your God; fear** [reverence] **not the gods of the Amorites, in whose land ye dwell':**
>
> **but ye have not obeyed my voice."** Judges 6:8-10 (KJV)

Nevertheless, upon their petition to the Lord, he sent an angel to Gideon, who was beating out wheat in the winepress. The angel addressed Gideon,

> > **"The LORD is with thee, thou mighty man of valour."**
>
> **Then Gideon said to the angel,**
>
> > **. . ."Oh my Lord, if the LORD be with us, why then is all this befallen us? and where be all his miracles which our fathers told us of . . .?"**
>
> **And the Lord looked upon him and said,**
>
> > **Go in this thy might . . . have not I sent thee?**
>
> Judges 6:12-14 (KJV)

The people had been derelict, and the Lord had turned away from them, precipitating bewildering misfortune. In distress, they cried out to the Lord. The Lord heard and appointed an unlikely deliverer.

Gideon's family was least in the tribe of Manasseh, and he was the least important in his father's house. But the Lord told him to go with what he had and begin the task, assuring him,

> **"Surely I will be with thee. . . ."** Judges 6:16 (KJV)

Gideon was hesitant, but he acted. That very same night, he destroyed the altar of Baal. Then he assembled an army to go up against the Midianites, the Amalekites, and the "sons of the east," who were camped in the valley of Jezreel (Armageddon).

The enemy assembled there numbered 135,000 men of war. They covered the valley floor like locusts, and their war animals were as numerous as the sand on the seashore. Gideon's army numbered just 32,000 men. Surprisingly, the Lord said to him . . .

. . ."The people that are with thee are too many. . . . therefore go to, proclaim in the ears of the people, saying,

'Whosoever is fearful and afraid, let him . depart. .'"
Judges 7:2-3 (KJV)

and 22,000 were excused, but 10,000 remained.

Stunningly, the Lord said the people were *still* too many, and he examined them at the water's edge. All who knelt to drink at the water's edge, lowering their head as a dog laps, were dismissed, but those who cupped the water in their hand, bringing it to their mouths – ever wary, ever vigilant, ever prepared – were allowed to remain; and

. . . the number of them that lapped, putting their hand to their mouth, were three hundred men. . . . Judges 7:6 (KJV)

With God and three-hundred wary, vigilant, prepared warriors, Gideon routed a well-equipped enemy that outnumbered his forces by four-hundred-fifty to one, oddly enough the same odds that Elijah had overcome.

*

Perhaps without the temple-based homage so rigidly fixed in the modern concept of Christianity, there's concern there'll be no people. There'll be people. There won't be as many, the fearful having been excused and the unprepared dismissed, but those remaining will be the only people both willing and able to enter the New Testament promised land and possess the mysterious kingdom of God.

Those wedded to the concept of the institutional Church, complete with dedicated Church structures and associated personal property, a stylized worship, and a hired clergy as a condition of their faith have Christianity as they want it, perhaps as they need it. They are true to the light within them. They would be unsuited to the unfamiliar first-century expression of Christianity. Only a relative few – quietly and urgently committed – will choose this way. It is prophesied by the map.

* * *

Anna comes forward with a small case in her hand, smiling warmly, that same smile in which I've basked for twelve gratifying years. We take the small elevator to the ground floor and step out into a warm, late morning Indian summer sun that feels splendid on the face and shoulders. There's a taxi waiting at the curb to carry us the ten blocks to the hospital. Anna and I hold hands, but speak little during the short drive. Then, my arm in hers for support, we walk through the same double doors we entered for the first time just twenty-two days ago.

I'm again assigned a hospital room, this time of necessity on 10-B, where we are to do nothing but wait. Occasionally, operating room personnel drop by the room, ask a few relevant questions, and then depart. In late afternoon, Dr. William Marshall, my thirty-three-year-old, prematurely-graying chief surgeon stops by wearing fresh, green operating room scrubs. As he sips casually on a cup of fruit juice, he tells me we are scheduled as soon as the operating room is properly prepared following the last surgery.

At seven o'clock in the evening, a gurney is wheeled into the room to transport me to the most dramatic and dangerous of all surgeries. I climb onto the gurney and hospital personnel drape me warmly and fasten straps over me. After having been stalled all day, things are moving swiftly now.

Anna leans over the gurney and appears above me. She smiles and kisses me good-bye. Her smile is one of confidence and the genuine expectation that she will see me again soon, but now, as quickly as she materialized above me, she's gone.

* * *

"Stand by the ways and see and ask for the ancient paths, where the good way is, and walk in it; and you shall find rest. . . ."

Jeremiah 6:16 (NASB)

Those who with good cause impugn Christianity and belittle the name and the concept of God and Jesus Christ because of the transparent failings of the Church might consider this: the failure doesn't rest with God or Jesus, for they are not necessarily Christian who wear the name Christian. If, as the apostle Paul said, one is not a Jew who is one outwardly, then neither is one a Christian who is one outwardly. He is a Christian who is one inwardly, whose cleansing is that of the heart, by the Spirit, and not of men, for his affirmation comes not from men, but from God.

> **"To what purpose is the multitude of your sacrifices unto me?"**

saith the LORD:

> **"I am full of the burnt offerings of rams and the fat of fed beasts; and I delight not in the blood of bullocks, or of lambs, or of he goats. When ye come to appear before me, who hath required this at your hand, to tread my courts? Bring no more vain oblations; incense [prayer] is an abomination unto me; the new moons and sabbaths, the calling of assemblies, I cannot away with; it is iniquity, even the solemn meeting. Your new moons and your appointed feasts my soul hateth: they are a trouble unto me; I am weary to bear them. And when ye spread forth your hands, I will hide mine eyes from you: yea, when ye make many prayers, I will not hear. . . . Wash you, make you clean . . . learn to do well; seek judgment, relieve the oppressed, judge the fatherless, plead for the widow."**
>
> Isaiah 1:11-17 (KJV)

* * *

The five-minute journey by way of the elevators and through the corridors and swinging doors is familiar to me. I see the ceiling lights flashing by overhead. I hear the low rumble of the gurney's wheels and the occasional thump of its rubber-bumpered edges coming into forceful contact with the swinging doors, thrusting them open and sliding by. And all this interspersed with the conventional chatter of hospital personnel going through another ordinary day's work.

While waiting for a service elevator to respond, a young hospital orderly, upon learning I'm being transported to this particularly surgery, pauses before sincerely wishing me good luck. I appreciate the manner of his gesture, which does not attempt to minimize or gloss over with false optimism the seriousness of my situation. As young as he is, he doesn't shrink from looking squarely into the eyes of a man who may well be dead within hours . . . and knows it.

I'm parked in a large room with holding areas and a station manned by three nurses. The room is chilly. I'm the only patient in this room. Pleasant, wisecracking hospital personnel wearing fresh, green operating room scrubs occasionally appear above my gurney and offer light, familiar humor.

My anesthesiologist, a diminutive, middle-aged woman with a charming British accent, introduces herself as Dr. Fletcher. Dr. Marshall puts his arm around her shoulder, smiling and telling me she is his favorite.

Death stands above me, whispering low
I know not what into my ear;
Of his strange language all I know
Is, there is not a word of fear.

Walter Savage Landor (1775-1864) *Epigrams*, c. *Death*

I'm still easy. No panic yet. I think to myself it's incredible I'm taking the whole thing so well.

* * *

Our revels now are ended. . . .
And, like the baseless fabric of this vision,
The cloud-capp'd towers, the gorgeous palaces,
The solemn temples . . . shall dissolve
And, like this insubstantial pageant faded,
Leave not a rack behind.

William Shakespeare, *The Tempest*, IV.i.l.48

Why did I spend all that time going to church all those years of my life? Was it to meet God? Was it to receive the Word of God? Was it to fellowship with those of the family of God? Did I do it to enhance my standing in the community-at-large? Did I actually believe I could use religion as a sort of lightning rod to ward off bolts of divine wrath? If in the end I could've answered in the affirmative to any of those questions, then by all means I would've continued going to church. There's no one who can summon into question the calling of another. There's no mending for that which isn't broken, no healing for that which isn't sick, no restitution for that which isn't lost, and no furtherance for that which has arrived. We can have no proof of any one position relating to the being and nature of God, the nature of bodies and spirits, souls, or any of the great truths of morality and religion, but for the one struggling to understand the inconsistency between expectation and experience, the theory invites patient consideration.

* * *

Still strapped to the same gurney that brought me down from 10-B, I'm wheeled into the operating room. I would've called it a chamber before calling it a room. It's even colder than the large, outer room where I'd waited, strapped on the gurney, perhaps twenty minutes. The chamber has a marvelous stereo system, with a volume and quality to match any disco of the 70's – and the music is blaring. I recognize the selection immediately. It's "Surfin' Bird," by The Trashmen. I can't believe I'm smiling. Within seconds the music is turned off, and I don't hear the stereo system again.

* * *

Dare to be true: nothing can need a lie;
A fault, which needs it most, grows two thereby.
George Herbert (1593-1633) *The Church Porch*, xiii

The theory needn't be dismissed with the notion that it's destructive of faith. On the contrary, the theory suggests a faith that dares to transform centuries of iconic Christian homage into a face-to-face, down-to-earth confrontation with the Christ in each man, woman, and child in the path of each believer.

St. Jerome was an early Church father who, whatever short-comings he may have possessed, gave this poignant advice, which would have been worthy of the messengers themselves:

> **"Others build churches, erect impressive columns, ornament doors with silver and ivory, and embellish altars with precious jewels. . . . But your task is other than these: to clothe Christ in the poor, to visit him in the sick, to feed him in the hungry, to welcome him in those who have no roof over their heads."**

* * *

I'm awed by the huge spotlights, as big as washtubs, by the polished surgical steel which comprises virtually every component of the room, and by the massive three-hundred-sixty degree, darkly-tinted glass molding at the ceiling, which conceals the gallery. This gallery glass is pitched out at a thirty degree angle from the upper portion of the gleaming walls, adding to my impression of this room as a diving chamber or bell.

I'm asked to assist in moving myself from the gurney to the operating table, which requires only the shifting of my weight using elbows, buttocks and heels. I'm stunned by the narrowness of the operating table. There's not even room to lay my arms by my side. It occurs to me that these guys have to get in close. My arms are stretched out perpendicular to my body and secured by Velcro straps to thin cross arms that extend from the table.

Depend upon it, Sir, when a man knows he is to be hanged in a fortnight, it concentrates his mind wonderfully.
Samuel Johnson (1709-1784) Boswell, *Life of Johnson*
(L. F. Powell's revision of G. B. Hill's edition), vol.iii, p.167, 19 Sept. 1777

A cap with a Velcro wrap is placed over my head, but not my eyes. I ask the busy, but accommodating operating personnel to wrap my cold feet. This is done immediately. Now the anesthesiologist with the charming British accent is behind my head, talking into my ear with calm, soothing words. I'm comfortable, still unafraid and not particularly anxious. I'm resigned.

As a hooded prisoner placed against the wall, hearing the rattle of the weaponry, I simply have no more choices. It's either this or else a miserable, short-lived existence followed by a ghastly death from major organ failure or variceal hemorrhaging. There is no longer any doubt about the necessity or timing of this decision.

* * *

Though all the winds of doctrine were let loose to play upon the earth, so Truth be in the field, we do injuriously by licensing and prohibiting to misdoubt her strength. Let her and Falsehood grapple; who ever knew Truth put to the worse, in a free and open encounter?
John Milton (1608-1674) *Areopagitica* (1644)

If modern Christianity is, in fact, the embodiment of the body and the bride of Christ as it purports to be, the theory will amount to no more than a pebble bouncing off of a Goliath. If it is without basis, it will manifest only as the inaudible croaking of a very small frog in a very big pond.

> **". . . if . . . of men, it will come to nothing. . . . but if it be of God, ye cannot overthrow it; lest haply ye be found even to fight against God."** Acts 5:38b-39 (KJV)

A new truth comes from the quarter whence it is not looked for and is always different from what's expected. It always begins in obscurity and is received with skepticism, and properly so. If it be worthy, it will become a power unobserved. Mockers will only serve to validate it.

> **Then said they,**
>
> > **"Come, and let us devise devices against Jeremiah; for the law shall not perish from the priest, nor counsel from the wise, nor the word from the prophet. Come, and let us smite him with the tongue, and let us not give heed to any of his words."** Jeremiah 18:18 (KJV)

The theory counsels wariness of those who aggressively attempt to protect the Church from perceived heresies when they are most responsible for and receiving the benefits of the promulgation of their particular brand of Christianity. One is ill-advised to accept the siren call of others on such matters, desiring the secrets of the record to be revealed by specialists such as those who repair our car or cap our teeth. Those who seek truth at fire sale prices become prey to doctrines and practices that serve the ambition of others. The wisdom and understanding of the ancient record is contracted to those engaged in a personal search for the kingdom of God.

> **". . . this is a rebellious people, false sons, sons who refuse to listen to the instruction of the Lord; who say to the seers,**
>
> > **'You must not see visions';**
>
> **and to the prophets,**
>
> > **'You must not prophesy to us what is right; speak to us pleasant words; prophesy illusions.'"**
>
> Isaiah 30:9-10 (NASB)

The great majority of those who currently elect active contemporary Christianity are fundamentally decent, virtuous men and women of sincere conviction who love and value the essence of Jesus, but . . .

One can live in the shadow of an idea without grasping it.
Elizabeth Bowen (1899-1973) *The Heat of the Day* (1949), ch.10

In arteriosclerotic conformity cultivated by my ecclesiastic and lay ancestors over the centuries, I had surely done so. And for my ignorance, my sacrifice had remained before the altar my hands had helped create, unclaimed and unacknowledged by God.

* * *

For the first time, I look up and concentrate on the tinted gallery glass a few feet above the heads of the operating room personnel. I'm struck by the soft, but unmistakable image I see with my uncorrected, nearsighted vision. A bearded man's body, partially draped in white from the waist to the ankles, arms extended perpendicular to the torso, the supporting structure visible only as it extends beyond the head, the feet and the knuckles.

Anxiety is increasing now, like that of a condemned prisoner strapped in the electric chair, waiting as prison personnel begin distancing themselves, not knowing whether the next sensation he'll experience will be the ringing of the wall phone with a life-giving reprieve or a lightning bolt of electricity propelling him into eternity.

In my youth I'd stood at the edge of the field with the wind blowing through my then thick, dark hair, watching the approaching squall line at evening, its lightning flashing along the dark horizon like distant artillery, its continuous thunder growling like the cannons of Sherman's advancing army. Now, at the moment of commitment, the panoply of life passes before me in a crescendo of sight and sensation:

As a boy stretched out on his back in the green, green grass of summer, I had watched thunderheads crown when reaching the frigid upper atmosphere, a wispy angel-hair halo enveloping the expanding upper reaches of the cloud.

As a young man, I had piloted my own light aircraft among those summer clouds, where in my youth the hawks flew. Throttling back, applying carburetor heat and allowing the propeller to windmill in the airstream, I'd glided through the canyons created by billowing cumulus with the wind rushing exhilaratingly past my face.

I had flown above Mt. McKinley on a remarkably clear, bitterly cold day and observed its rugged, unearthly, snow-covered terrain from a platform until recently available only to eagles.

Aboard a darkened Lockheed Electra deadheading from Hartford to New York on an astonishingly clear night, I'd pressed my face to the window at midnight. Alone in the cabin as it passed through a thousand feet on its downwind leg to La Guardia Airport, all of Manhattan, aglow with its night lights, was visible to my astonished eyes, so close it seemed as though I could reach out and touch the familiar city skyline.

I had witnessed in a single image a towering thunderhead that only minutes earlier had spawned a killer tornado. A mushroom-shaped cloud of awesome dimensions, its base spread out over the darkened landscape below, emitting flashes of lightning like fireflies on a June night in the summer of my youth. Its massive column and huge, expanding crown constantly discharged cloud-to-cloud bolts of lightning. And all of this was illuminated by a full moon which bathed in spectral light the enormous cloud beyond the silvery wing tip of the rain delayed Boeing 707 that was flying nonstop from Atlanta to Memphis with a handful of sleeping passengers at two o'clock in the morning.

I had skied the Colorado peak from its windswept upper reaches, barren except for the lightning-blasted skeletons of a few bold spruces, to a base lush with deep, green forests. This I'd done with nothing but the wind on my face and the sound of my skis racing over the surface of the packed snow.

I had scuba dived beneath the Caribbean Sea to witness the colors and wonders of the coral reef.

I had known the despair of a hopeless relationship only to be reborn in the love of a good woman.

I had known the heady intoxication of winning and the bitter disappointment of losing.

I'd known the deceitful satisfaction when all men had spoken well of me, and I'd known the biting impoverishment of rejection.

I had known the quiet desperation of all men.

Now it's time to let go. I'm nearing the end of the journey that began with Chester Eakins' departure for the war in the summer of '44 and continued right through the corridors and the swinging doors of Presbyterian-University Hospital. Here on the operating table with finality close and very real, mesmerized by the reflection in the gallery glass, I savor the moment I first perceived the epiphanic Jesus, and I feel the liberating immunity that lies just beyond the letting go, just beyond the myriad distractions of a frantic existence, a gift from the image that – imperceptible to the wise – patiently awaits the blank curiosity of a child.

I feel a warm, relaxing glow. The momentary anxiety is melting away, just as I seem to be melting away, flowing off the table. I'm calm again. That which is within – the silence, the assuasive, amplifying silence that has served me so long and so well – comforts me, shielding me from the enveloping darkness. And I am not alone.

EPILOGUE

The Christ That Is To Be
And not in age I bud again,
After so many deaths I live and write;
I once more smell the dew and rain,
And relish versing: O, my only Light,
It cannot be
That I am he
On whom Thy tempests fell all night.
George Herbert (1593-1633) *The Flower*

It has been by far the hardest thing I've ever done, that journey into the maelstrom and the unexpected expulsion through the surge. I didn't take the path voluntarily, but in my heart I willed the passage and the promontory from which I now see what eluded me then. Courage might have failed me had I been able to comprehend the wilderness which lay between my centuries-old, conditioned blindness – that which had been my confident vision – and the cleansing blindness that at last proved to be my consummate sight.

> **The LORD hath chastened me sore: but he hath not given me over unto death. . . . I shall not die, but live, and declare the works of the LORD.** Psalms 118:18, 17 (KJV)

*

The little wartime congregation of which Helen Eakins was a charter member is still active, having moved into a newer, larger building several decades ago.

Chester Eakins survived his first heart attack at age forty-two. He died as a result of his third heart attack in 1973. He was fifty-seven years old.

Helen Eakins was married thirty-nine years and widowed thirty-seven years. She passed away quietly, simply worn out from the years, in 2010 at the age of ninety-four.

Gail Estes, Helen's sister, died of an apparent stroke in 1981. She was sixty-two years old. Gail's husband, the raucous ex-Marine Harlan Estes, survived her, passing away in 1995. Helen Eakins never got over the twist of fate that took Gail first, instead of the older, hard-living Harlan Estes. She grieved over losing Gail until her own death, twenty-nine years later.

Jean married her college sweetheart in 1954. Now surrounded by children and grandchildren, she and her husband have lived in Little Rock since 1955.

Dwayne Lee Penry and I remained closer than brothers, continuing our adventures together throughout the remainder of his life. He died in his sleep of apparent cardiac arrest in the summer of '84, only forty-two years old and with a Pernell Roberts physique and bearing. To my knowledge, he'd never been sick a day in his life. He left a wife, two teenagers, and a preschooler.

Charlie Gee Penry, mechanical engineer and snake-killer *par excellence*, became a corporate jet pilot. Long retired now, he lives today with his wife in Middle Tennessee, close to his children and grandchildren.

Uncle Arthur and Aunt Lois, having been born within days of each other early in the twentieth-century, died of unrelated natural causes, also within days of each other, in the summer of '69.

Doc Davis, the former snake-oil salesman, lived several more years and – with humor more appropriate to the time – swore he intended to die in the electric chair at the age of 103 for raping the homecoming queen. He died short of that goal at a testimonial given in his honor, collapsing in his chair at the head table, his face buried in his plate.

Of school yard experiences, I increased in both stature and playground savvy. Just a few years following the humiliations of the first-grade school playground, I stood six-foot-two and weighed 183 pounds, a varsity high school football team tri-captain in Arkansas' largest athletic conference.

I don't know what became of Jody Tremain, my first-grade tormentor. Following that first-grade year, I never saw or heard of him again.

Buddy, the colored man who worked side-by-side with Elijah Roy and whose family enjoyed evenings of grainy television with my grandparents in the backwoods of the wild White River Bottoms, died soon thereafter in a tragic logging accident. While felling timber in the woods alone, he was penned beneath a fallen tree trunk. An inopportune brush fire, probably ignited as a result of the accident, got to him before the search party did. Anticipating his own death by the fire, Buddy had taken his wallet out of his pocket and tucked it beneath his body. Facing his own imminent death, he was the responsible husband and father, thinking of the needs of his family. As he planned, the fire failed to destroy the little money his wife and twin daughters would need.

Elijah and Lila Roy lived and worked in the deep backwoods for twelve years. Advancing age and failing health finally forced him to retire closer to civilization. He ended a bedfast invalid, broken in health and financially dependent upon a small Social Security pension and the generosity of his children and his sons-in-law. In 1962, after suffering several debilitating strokes, he died in his bed in a rented cottage across the river in Clarksdale, Mississippi. Before her death in 1979, I asked Lila Roy about his precipitous decision to leave the Missouri Bootheel and all he had known to go to the White River Bottoms. What had motivated him to so do? I was convinced by her response that she really didn't know. He was that reticent a man.

Rebekah graduated from the university, took a job on the East Coast, married, and began a family. She now lives with her husband and three children in Fayetteville, Arkansas.

Young Jared graduated with honors from the flagship state university in Columbia. He married a charming Slovak girl in 2005 and is the father of two sons. He lives and works abroad.

We long ago lost the old Pekinese to the years.

Of perhaps fifty patients from all over the world who were in the unit designated 10-B at Presbyterian-University Hospital in the autumn of '88, Anna and I came to know fifteen well. Fourteen of these were eventually discharged to their homes. Of the original group, twelve were dead within three years, including the young would-be-missionary who, while recovering from that desperate surgery, came to my third-floor pre-op bedside to pray for my deliverance when I was yet a stranger to him. Despite his wholesome appearance that day, he became the first of the twelve, dying just a few months out from surgery without ever being discharged from Presbyterian-University Hospital. The remaining three, including me, are well enough.

And Anna? Anna and I are still together.

* * *

Who would has heard Sordello's story told.

Robert Browning (1812-1889) *Sordello*, bk.vi, l.886

The ancient Hebrew record must be its own defense. The power of it can never be proved if it isn't felt. The authority of it can never be supported unless it is obvious.

If the theory be heresy to some, surely . . .

To pluck the mask from the face of the Pharisee
is not to lift an impious hand to the Crown of Thorns.

Charlotte Bronte (1816-1855) *Jane Eyre*, Preface to 2nd edition, 1847

Fortunate and blessed are those that have true wisdom. And second to them, not the many that think they have it, but the few that are sensible of the defects and imperfections of their Christian endeavor, and know that they have it not.

Ring out a slowly dying cause,
And ancient forms of party strife;
Ring in the nobler modes of life,
With sweeter manners, purer laws.

. . .

Ring in the valiant man and free,
The larger heart, the kindlier hand;
Ring out the darkness of the land;
Ring in the Christ that is to be.

Alfred, Lord Tennyson (1809-1892) *In Memoriam A.H.H.* (1850), cvi

To the believer to whom all seems lost, except a little life, the theory has been presented and its defense advanced. Having given script to the theory, I've kept my vow. Having sealed the missive and cast it into the swiftly moving flood, as Dwayne and I did as children, I've completed the mission. Now I, too, have been true to the light within me.

*

Iamque opus exegi, quod nec Iovis ira,
nec ignis,
Nec poterit ferrum,
nec edax abolere vetustas.
And now I have finished the work, which neither the wrath of Jove, nor fire, nor the sword, nor devouring age shall be able to destroy.
Ovid (43 BCE-17 CE) *Metamorphoses*, xv.871

I wait now, almost breathless, as when a child I waited for the thunder following the flash, as when on that operating table, helpless and defeated, gazing upon that mesmerizing image in the gallery glass. And I shall not be cruelly disappointed.

One thing I have asked from the Lord, that I shall seek; that I may dwell in the house of the Lord all the days of my life, to behold the beauty of the Lord, and to inquire in His temple.
Psalms 27:4 (NASB, KJV)

Even so, come Lord Jesus. Revelation 22:20b (KJV)

ENDNOTES

[1] Ralph Waldo Emerson (1803-1882), *Essays: Self-Reliance* (1841)
[2] Bernard of Chartres, d. ca.1130, John of Salisbury, *Metalogicon* (1159), bk.III., ch.iv
[3] Lois Lenski (aka Leona Landon) *Cotton In My Sack*, Lippincott, 1949
[4] See Ecclesiastes 1:4-7
[5] See Ezekiel 1:16b
[6] See Matthew 4:4 (Luke 4:4); 4:7; 4:10 (Luke 4:8); 11:10 (Luke 7:27); 21:13 (Luke 19:46); 26:24 (Mark 14:21); 26:31; Mark 7:6; 9:12-13; 14:27; Luke 24:46; John 6:45
[7] See Acts 5:34-39
[8] See Acts 22:3
[9] See Matthew 16:17
[10] See Matthew 23:35; Genesis 4:8; 2 Chronicles 24:21
[11] William Shakespeare, *Hamlet*, III,i.56
[12] See 2 Corinthians 12:7
[13] See 2 Corinthians 11:23b-28
[14] See Job 24:12
[15] See 1 Corinthians 3:15b
[16] See Acts 8:1b
[17] John 4:21 (KJV)
[18] See Mark 6:14-29
[19] See Luke 24:13
[20] See Luke 7:2-6a
[21] See Luke 23:32-33,39-43
[22] See Luke 18:9-14
[23] See Jude 4,11-13
[24] See 2 Peter 2:15
[25] See Revelation 2:14
[26] See Samuel Butler (1835-1902) *The Way of All Flesh*, ch.15
[27] See Isaiah 27:8; Hosea 13:15

KJV	King James Version
NASB	New American Standard Bible

ABOUT THE AUTHOR

James Earle was born and raised in Mississippi County, Arkansas, just north of Memphis on U.S. Highway 61. A graduate of the Blytheville High School Class of '57, he was there, by dumb luck perfectly positioned, in what has to have been the Golden Age of Adolescence.

After graduating from college in 1961, he spent the next sixteen years in residential, farm, and commercial real estate finance and investment analysis. He was a faculty member at a regional state university – from which he is currently retired – throughout the eventful '80s.

His boyhood role model was screen actor John Wayne, but he has followed the life and writings of Dietrich Bonhoeffer since 1992. Neither a brilliant theologian like the quiet, intense Bonhoeffer nor a religious enthusiast like the modern Evangelicals, he considers himself what nineteenth-century Darwinian scientist Thomas Henry Huxley referred to as a "Sunday scholar." His Christian persona is probably closer to that of the rough-hewn, pre-Pentecost Simon Peter.

He lists among his favorite poetry Thomas Hardy's "The Impercipient" and has admired evangelist Billy Graham for decades.

He and his wife of thirty-seven years, Anne, live in Willard, Missouri.

www.ingramcontent.com/pod-product-compliance
Lightning Source LLC
Chambersburg PA
CBHW021126020426
42331CB00005B/642

* 9 7 8 0 6 1 5 8 6 7 2 6 7 *